THE POWER OF THE 10

ALSO BY REV. DR. ARLENE CHURN

The End Is Just the Beginning:
Lessons in Grieving for African Americans

BROADWAY BOOKS

NEW YORK

THE
POWER
OF THE 10

HOW TO EMBRACE THE COMMANDMENTS, HANDLE STRESS, AND ACHIEVE SUCCESS

REV. DR. ARLENE CHURN

Book design by Gretchen Achilles

Library of Congress Cataloging-in-Publication Data
Churn, Arlene H.
   The power of the 10 : how to embrace the commandments, handle stress, and achieve success / by Arlene Churn. — 1st ed.
      p. cm.
1. Ten commandments—Criticism, interpretation, etc.
2. Success—Biblical teaching. 3. Success—Religious aspects—Christianity. I. Title.
BS1285.52.C48 2008
241.5'2—dc22
2008021923

ISBN 978-0-7679-1016-3

PRINTED IN THE UNITED STATES OF AMERICA

10 9 8 7 6 5 4 3 2 1

First Edition

This book is lovingly dedicated to

David Poindexter, my spiritual son;

Dexter Martin, my special nephew;

Rev. Dr. Robert Perry,
my personal pastor and cherished friend;

Martin Kardon, Esq.,
my attorney, who was my source of
inspiration and motivation;

Delores A. Rush,
the wind beneath my wings.

The world is too much with us; late and soon,

Getting and spending, we lay waste our powers.

—WILLIAM WORDSWORTH

And God spake all these words, saying,

I *am* the Lord thy God, which have brought thee out of the land of Egypt, out of the house of bondage.

Thou shalt have no other gods before me.

Thou shalt not make unto thee any graven image, or any likeness *of any thing* that *is* in heaven above, or that *is* in the earth beneath, or that *is* in the water under the earth:

Thou shalt not bow down thyself to them, nor serve them: for I the Lord thy God *am* a jealous God, visiting the iniquity of the fathers upon the children unto the third and fourth *generation* of them that hate me;

And showing mercy unto thousands of them that love me, and keep my commandments.

Thou shalt not take the name of the Lord thy God in vain; for the Lord will not hold him guiltless that taketh his name in vain.

Remember the sabbath day, to keep it holy.

Six days shalt thou labour, and do all thy work:

But the seventh day *is* the sabbath of the Lord thy God: *in it* thou shalt not do any work, thou, nor thy son, nor thy daughter, thy manservant, nor thy maidservant, nor thy cattle, nor thy stranger that *is* within thy gates:

For *in* six days the Lord made heaven and earth, the sea, and all that in them *is*, and rested the seventh day: wherefore the Lord blessed the sabbath day, and hallowed it.

Honour thy father and thy mother: that thy days may be long upon the land which the Lord thy God giveth thee.

Thou shalt not kill.

Thou shalt not commit adultery.

Thou shalt not steal.

Thou shalt not bear false witness against thy neighbour.

Thou shalt not covet thy neighbour's house, thou shalt not covet thy neighbour's wife, nor his manservant, nor his maidservant, nor his ox, nor his ass, nor any thing that *is* thy neighbour's.

CONTENTS

THE POWER OF THE 10

10 IS A POWERFUL NUMBER

"To whatever side you turn, you are forced to ac-knowledge your own ignorance and the boundless power of the Creator."

—VOLTAIRE, *Letters on England*

In the 2006–07 television season there was a quiz program called "The Power of Ten" in which contestants were asked to guess the percentage of people who agreed or disagreed with a particular statement. They were rewarded in increments of $10,000 for each right answer, with the potential of winning $10,000 to the tenth power, or $1,000,000.

I thought about the title of that program, and then I thought about how often we are asked to rate something "on a scale of one to ten," with ten representing perfection. Ten is a powerful number, and God's commandments provide us with all the power we need not just to survive but to succeed in every aspect of life.

Some people think about the commandments in terms of "thou shalt nots"—in other words, things that are forbidden, things from which we must abstain. But I would suggest that shalts and shalt nots are nothing more than a matter of perspective. Each one has its opposite. So, if we're told thou shalt not commit adultery, we can just as easily flip that around and say, you shall be faithful to your spouse. Or, if we're told, thou shalt not steal, what that really means is that we should live honestly. If we look at the commandments from that perspective, it becomes clear that they are not arbitrary rules meant to constrict and restrict us but rather guidelines for living a good life. If we abstain from thoughts and habits that weaken our connection with God, we will be thinking and acting in ways that give us greater access to His power.

How sad then that so many of our young people are totally ignorant of these simple guidelines. In years past, reciting the commandments was an integral part of the weekly worship service. Each commandment was read aloud and the congregation would respond,

"Lord, have mercy upon us and incline our heart to keep this law." Now they have been completely eliminated from many services, they no longer appear in public places, and are seldom on display even in modern churches. Not so long ago, I scolded a group of young people who were cursing and taking the Lord's name in vain, and when I reminded them of the third commandment, "thou shalt not take the name of the Lord thy God in vain," they had no idea what I was talking about. They had absolutely no knowledge of the Ten Commandments. This is a sad commentary on the world we live in.

We hear in First John Chapter 5, "his commandments are not grievous," because "when we love God, and keep his commandments" we also "love the children of God" (1 John 5:2–3). But what exactly does that mean? It means that by obeying His commandments we are showing love and kindness to our fellow men, since we are all the children of God. If you doubt that, just think about how peaceful the world would be if everyone everywhere lived by these simple rules.

Jesus makes that clear when, in Matthew 22, he is addressing the Pharisees and someone asks him,

"Master, which *is* the great commandment in the law?" and Jesus replies, "Thou shalt love the Lord thy God with all thy heart, and with all thy soul, and with all thy mind. This is the first and great commandment. And the second *is* like unto it, Thou shalt love thy neighbor as thyself" (Matthew 22: 36–39).

Ecclesiastes 3:1 tells us that "to everything there is a season and a time for every purpose," and the purpose of God's giving us the Ten Commandments was, first of all, so that we could all live in peace and tranquillity with one another. And also so that we could look to them as guidelines for living a successful, prosperous, and happy life.

We must remember that the children of Israel, and particularly Moses, who personally received the commandments, were already well aware and had firsthand experience of God's power. Not only did He appear to Moses in the burning bush while Moses was living in exile, He also proved His power by inflicting ten plagues upon the Egyptians and by parting the Red Sea so that the Israelites could escape. In fact, God kept every covenant He made with the Israelites. He promised to deliver them out of bondage and into the land of milk and honey, and all He asked of them in return was that they accept Him as their one true God and live by these ten clear and simple rules.

They also felt the power of His wrath at firsthand when they momentarily doubted Him and feared that He would not be able to protect them against the strength of the people of Canaan (Numbers 13:31). Those who doubted Him were not allowed to enter the Promised Land, while those who followed Joshua and Caleb, the only ones who did not doubt Him, were allowed to enter under His protection. Sadly, those who doubted Him had apparently forgotten that He is omnipotent and omnipresent, and that He would be aware of their every thought, word, and deed.

And again, in the Book of Chronicles, we see the power that comes from obeying His Commandments. In 2 Chronicles 7:17–20, God says to Solomon:

> *If thou wilt walk before me, as David thy father walked, and do according to all that I have commanded thee, and shalt observe my statutes and my judgments; Then will I stablish the throne of thy kingdom, according as I have covenanted with David thy*

father, saying, There shall not fail thee a man to be ruler in Israel. But if ye turn away, and forsake my statutes and my commandments, which I have set before you, and shall go and serve other gods, and worship them; Then will I pluck them up by the roots out of my land which I have given them; and this house, which I have sanctified for my name, will I cast out of my sight.

Solomon did as God commanded, and thus, we are told:

And Solomon reigned in Jerusalem over all Israel forty years.

And Solomon slept with his fathers, and he was buried in the city of David his father: and Rehoboam his son reigned in his stead.

How sad, then, to see people today still rejecting and rebelling against obedience to God's commandments. God was extremely explicit when He set down these rules for living, but many people, it seems, hate being told what to do. What these people don't realize, however, is that He didn't give us this list of shalts and shalt nots just to be arbitrary. The power of the commandments lies not in getting us to blindly follow a set of rules; their true power lies in connecting us with our Godly heritage. As we are told in Ephesians 6:10, "Be strong in the Lord, and in the power of his might." Or, in the words of a favorite Christian hymn, "Oh! What peace we often forfeit, Oh! What needless pain we bear, all because we do not carry everything to God in prayer" ("What a Friend We Have in Jesus," Joseph Scriven, 1855). Without the moral structure and power they provide, our lives are out of order.

I'm sure you will agree when I say that we're living in turbulent times. On the one hand, we seem to have more of everything than ever before—iPods, Black-Berries, camera phones, SUVs, and labor-saving devices of every kind. And yet, we also live in a war zone. We are fighting wars on all fronts—the war on poverty, the war on drugs, the war on violence, and the war on discrimination. More than ever these days we need to reconnect with our Lord by following the path He laid out for us, but a lot of people don't see it that way. When things go wrong, they react like Job's wife, who, in the midst of her husband's suffering, told him to "curse God, and die" (Job 2:9). But Job knew better. In his darkest time, he says, "Neither have I gone back from the commandment of his lips; I have esteemed the words of his mouth more than my necessary *food*" (Job 23:12). He never lost his faith, and as we are told in Hebrews 11:6, "without faith *it is* impossible to please *him*. . . ." But, on the other hand, "They that wait upon the Lord shall renew *their* strength; they shall mount up with wings as eagles; they shall run, and not be weary; *and* they shall walk, and not faint" (Isaiah 40:31).

We need to remember that man's first sin was not the act of eating the forbidden fruit; it was the act of disobedience to God. As Samuel told King Saul, "Hath the Lord as great delight in burnt offerings and sacrifices, as in obeying the voice of the Lord? Behold, to obey is better than sacrifice, and to hearken than the fat of rams" (1 Samuel 15:22).

God knew that we mortals needed strong guidelines to help us avoid making mistakes, because, fallible as we are, one mistake often leads to another until we are sliding down a slippery slope into sin. We sin in thought, word, or deed, but because we are all human, we are all guilty of sinning at one time or another. Sin is the great human equalizer.

Sin is generally defined as a transgression of moral law, and if we look to God as our moral guidepost, that means we sin each and every time we disobey any of His laws. There are sins of omission (a failure to do something) and sins of commission (doing something we shouldn't). There are venial or less serious sins, and deadly or mortal sins.

Although there is no specific listing of the seven deadly or mortal sins in the Bible, they were codified by Pope Gregory the Great in the sixth century AD. If we look at his list, we'll see that each one can be viewed as resulting more or less directly from a failure to obey one of God's commandments.

Lust leads to adultery.

Greed, *Gluttony*, and *Envy* are all forms of covetousness, leading us to desire more than we have or need.

Sloth, in its original sense, was defined as a failure to enjoy the goodness of God and the World He created, which can also be seen as a violation of His commandment to have no other gods before Him.

Wrath, or anger, leads to killing, stealing, bearing false witness, and any number of related ways of disobeying Him.

And *Pride* is an attempt to make ourselves more important than Him, which is, of course, putting another god before Him.

Are you risking mortal sin by failing to live up to God's commandments? Do you have a problem living by God's rules? Let's look at each one in turn and see what those problems might be. Perhaps once you understand their meaning and purpose more clearly, you'll be better able to embrace them and be less tempted to rebel against them.

CHAPTER ONE

"THOU SHALT HAVE NO OTHER GODS BEFORE ME"

EXODUS 20:3

> *Tell them, I AM, Jehovah said*
> *To Moses; while earth heard in dread,*
> *And, smitten to the heart,*
> *At once above, beneath, around,*
> *All Nature, without voice or sound,*
> *Replied, O LORD THOU ART.*
>
> —CHRISTOPHER SMART, *Song to David*

That seems clear and simple enough. But still people are constantly looking for little gods to fulfill their little needs. Too often we replace the god of need with the god of greed. We replace the god of love with the god of hate. We want a god who will support our causes and destroy our enemies. But these little gods, in the end, can't and won't help us because, as God said, "I am alpha and omega" (Revelation 22:13)—the beginning and the end, omnipotent and omnipresent. Everything comes from God and nothing will outlast Him.

When I speak with people who challenge God's position as the Supreme Being, I ask them who then made the mountains and the rivers? Who created the earth? And they, of course, are at a loss for an answer. They have no alternative explanation for the miracle of creation. There is no little god they can present who can say, "I did it." There is no little god who can claim that power or authority, because all these little gods are manmade.

THE BATTLE OF BAAL AND ELIJAH—
THE FAILURE OF A GOD ALTERNATIVE

The Bible, as well as our history books, is filled with stories of alternative gods. But not one of them has ever been known to step up to the plate in our hour of need. Jezebel, for example, served the god Baal and influenced her husband, Ahab, to worship him as well.

But when it came to a showdown between the true and living God of Joshua and Baal, Baal failed miserably.

Baal was thought to be the god in charge of the elements, the one with the power to send rain to earth, but one day the prophet Elijah appeared before Ahab and announced that it would not rain for a long time, not until he, Elijah, caused the rain to come. As time passed, the drought worsened and Ahab blamed Elijah for the rivers and creeks drying up and his people going hungry. At last Elijah returned, and Ahab accused him of having caused all Israel's troubles. But no, said Elijah, you are the cause "in that ye have forsaken the commandments of the Lord, and thou has followed Baalim" (1 Kings 18:18).

Elijah commanded Ahab to gather the people of Israel and the 450 prophets of Baal on Mount Carmel, and then asked the people, "How long halt ye between two opinions? if the Lord *be* God, follow him: but if Baal, *then* follow him" (1 Kings 18:21). When the people had no answer, Elijah announced that there would be a contest to see which was the real god. He told the prophets to bring two animals for sacrifice, one to Jehovah and the other to Baal.

The prophets built their altar and sacrificed their animal and began to pray to Baal. From morning to noon they kept shouting for him to appear while Elijah taunted them. "Cry aloud: for he *is* a god; either he is talking, or he is pursuing, or he is in a journey, *or* peradventure he sleepeth, and must be awaked" (1 Kings 18:27).

In the end, of course, Baal did not help them. But the true God, the God of the commandments, stepped up right on time and ended the drought, proving once more that He was, indeed, the alpha and omega, the all-powerful.

HE IS A GOD OF MERCY AND COMPASSION

In return for our obedience God said He would show "mercy unto thousands of them that love me, and keep my commandments" (Exodus 20:6). But if He is merciful, why then is there so much violence, so many vindictive and spiteful acts in the world? Whenever something goes terribly wrong, we question God— How could He do this to us? Or else we question His

very existence—If there were a God, He would not allow such evil to exist. But we must remember that
when God created man, He made it very clear that we
would have free will. We aren't zombies, nor did He
wish us to be. He didn't say that He would *make* us believe or follow His laws. Instead, we live both by His
direct will as outlined in the commandments and by
His permissive will, which is made clear in the many
accounts of the ways in which His people disobeyed
Him. God wants us to love Him voluntarily and unconditionally. He wants us to love Him with every
fiber of our being, and any disobedience of His commandments will cause catastrophe, chaos, confusions,
and sadness. The wages of sin is death.

Paul, in his epistle to the Romans (Romans 1:28-
32), makes clear both that man's transgressions are
performed of his own free will and that God punishes us when we transgress against His commands:
"And even as they did not like to retain God in *their*
knowledge, God gave them over to a reprobate mind,
to do those things which are not convenient; Being
filled with all unrighteousness, fornication, wicked-
ness, covetousness, maliciousness; full of envy, murder,

debate, deceit, malignity; whisperers, backbiters, haters of God, despiteful, proud, boasters, inventors of evil things, disobedient to parents, Without understanding, covenant-breakers, without natural affection, implacable, unmerciful: Who knowing the judgment of God, that they which commit such things are worthy of death, not only do the same, but have pleasure in them that do them."

But when things do go wrong as a result of the choices we make, God is looking upon us with compassion, as if to say, "If only you'd obeyed me, these things never would have happened."

GOD IS LOVE

Yes, God loves us. In fact, He loves us enough to have given us His only begotten son, who then gave his life for our sins. In John 21 Jesus, arisen from the grave, appears to his disciples and asks Simon Peter three times, "lovest thou me?" And when Peter replies three times in the affirmative, each time Jesus says, "feed my sheep." In other words, Jesus wanted Peter to serve him only if he loved him. Loving God is the prerequisite to our call to service and to serving others.

The Bible uses the word *agape* to define divine, unconditional, self-sacrificing, active, volitional, and thoughtful love. That's the love God gives and that He asks of us. Divine love is not only a commandment but a commitment. And remember that when Jesus reiterates the kind of love God expects from us in Matthew he adds a codicil: "Thou shalt love thy neighbor as thyself" (Matthew 22:39).

In other words, we demonstrate our love of God by loving our fellow man, who is, after all, made in God's image. That kind of love has enormous power. And yet, we give love a bad name by neglecting to live up to the responsibilities—the commitments—it requires. We say we love our parents, and yet we can't even find the time to stay in touch, much less to care for them as they have cared for us. We turn our back on those less fortunate within our own community, as well as the global community of man.

Perhaps worst of all, however, we make choices about which of our neighbors we do or do not choose to love. In too many communities where racial tensions rule, the "n" word is not neighbor but a racial epithet hurled in hate, the direct opposite of the love God requires His children to embrace. Nor are African Americans innocent of spewing vicious names in return. The hatred then spreads so that every ethnic and racial group is in a state of constant combat with those whom the Lord has admonished us to love. These violations of God's law are handed down from one generation to the next, and all parents need to teach their children the true meaning of God's great commandment.

We also subvert the kind of love God commanded of us when we confuse love with lust and with greed. We are told in The Epistle of James 1:15: "When lust hath conceived, it bringeth forth sin: and sin, when it is finished, bringeth forth death." It may not necessarily be physical death but rather the living death that results from enslavement. Lust and greed may be sexual. You may covet a person's body to the point where you want to own that person, in which case you diminish not only the object of your lust but also yourself, because you both become slaves to your unholy desire. But lust may also manifest as the desire for material goods or as jealousy of another person's looks or youth or wealth or possessions, any one of which will, in the end, result in your own diminishment because they supplant what is, in fact, true love, the love that God commanded us to give only unto Him. Whatever it is that we lust after becomes a little god whom we worship before the true God.

There's a daily African American radio program appropriately called *Love, Lust, and Lies*, because lust does cause us to lie. We lie to the one who is the object of our lust by claiming to "love" that person, but, in truth, when we lust after someone or something, our feelings are purely selfish, whereas real love is purely selfless, caring, kind, and sharing—as the love God has for us.

Let me share with you the story of Marcy, a twenty-year-old college student who was extremely confused about the difference between lust and love. Marcy's stepmother, Amanda, almost literally dragged her to me for counseling when she found out that Marcy had contracted a sexually transmitted disease. When Amanda asked Marcy with whom she had been intimate, her response was, "Lots of guys. I can't remember them all." Needless to say, Amanda was horrified, and also terrified of how Marcy's father would react to the news. "He thought all those boys were just puppy-love flings," she said, "and now I find out that you are really like a dog in heat."

In counseling, Marcy admitted that she'd been sexually active since the age of fourteen. She liked having sex, she said, and so did her multiple male partners. "It makes me feel good," she confessed sheepishly. The boys told her she was "hot," and she loved having that reputation. Foolishly, she believed they all loved her, and, of course, her popularity made her girlfriends jealous, which she also enjoyed.

When I asked her to define love and tell me whom she loved, she spoke of loving her parents (her father had married Amanda when Marcy was just seven, and she knew they both loved her) and her grandparents. She loved being a college student, she loved having her own car, and she loved clothes. She was also in total denial about her health problem and said she believed her doctor was simply trying to scare her into abstaining from sex. To which my response was, "Don't you think it's a little too late for that?"

I told Marcy in no uncertain terms that she was lustful, not loving, and that she needed to understand the meaning of real love and how to demonstrate it. I explained to her that when God created Eve, it was so that she would be a helpmeet and companion to Adam, not his sexual plaything. The love between a man and a woman should be binding, unconditional, and exclusive. Lust, on the other hand, does not bind, rather it destroys the bonds of marriage and relationships.

A few days after our first session, Marcy arrived at my office downcast and weepy. I asked her what was wrong, and she said that when she'd told some of the young men who called her that she was unable to have sex because of a "medical problem," the responses she received ranged from, "Well, if you're knocked up it isn't mine," to, "Call me when you get your freak back." Their selfishness and lack of concern made her conscious for the first time how little they really cared for her. Although I made Marcy aware of her obligation to inform her partners of her disease, she reluctantly admitted that she didn't remember all their names and had no way to get in touch with many of them.

In her shame, she was convinced that her father no longer loved her and that Amanda felt betrayed because Marcy had lied to her about her sexual activities. She'd also confided in one of her friends, and word of her problem had spread so that she now felt like an outcast among her peers. "Nobody loves me. I just want to die," she wailed.

Although attending church had been very much a part of her upbringing, and she enjoyed the songs and the sermons, she also believed (or thought she believed) that her life was her own to live as she saw fit. Now, however, she felt dirty and foolish. I realized that Marcy desperately needed to find her spiritual connection to the unconditional and forgiving love of God. She also needed to forgive herself, so I gave her several affirmations to repeat on a daily basis until she actually believed the words she was saying. In life coaching, I encourage my clients to speak and think things into being, for it is written in Proverbs 23:7, "As he thinketh in his heart, so *is* he." If we think of God as love

and of ourselves as His loving creations, we bring lo,
into our lives. Marcy's affirmations were:

God made me and He loves me.

I am sorry for my behavior and hurting and
disappointing those who love me.

I make no excuses or blame anyone for my selfish
indulgence.

I must forgive myself daily for using my body for
the wrong reason.

There is goodness in me and I want it to shine for
others to see.

I need God's intervention in my life and His
divine forgiveness.

I want to be made whole!

Because she was still feeling isolated, I also placed
Marcy in a therapy group comprised of people who
had lived their lives however they saw fit and then
been totally blindsided by a crisis.

One of these people was Brandon, a twenty-nine-year-old CPA with athletic good looks. Brandon loved himself more than anything in the world and expected others to feel the same way. He loved his good hair, he loved his height, and he was crazy about his light brown skin. His schedule of personal maintenance included weekly manicures and pedicures and, of course, he was a devotee of the health club. All in all, he loved himself too much to have any love left over for anyone else.

Brandon believed he could handle anything that came along, and he had no sympathy for failures or compassion for the problems of others. In other words, he was a total egomaniac. Brandon was a self-described "recreational drug user," but, of course, he could handle that, too. And he did, until his firm did a random, unannounced drug test and Brandon failed. He was suspended without pay and told that he would have to undergo counseling and be tested weekly when he returned to work.

Brandon was furious and didn't think he needed any "stupid counseling." But he did need the income from his high-paying job. It did, however, take a few weeks for him to get himself to counseling because by then his recreational drug use had escalated into a full-blown addiction. Then, once he got there, he had to be constantly reminded that the purpose of the group was not to listen to him talk about his self-proclaimed success and "control" of the situation.

After missing a couple of sessions, Brandon showed up one day looking awful. His hair was matted, he was unshaved and also apparently unwashed. Silent at first, he finally burst out, "Damn it, I need help!" And then, without any prodding, he began to tell his story. His parents were dead and he was estranged from his brother and two sisters. All men (himself excepted) were punks and pimps, and he'd never had a real relationship with a woman because they were all flakes. He didn't want children because he'd have to provide for them and their momma, which would put a cramp in his extravagant lifestyle. He believed that only weak people prayed, because the strong were able to take care of themselves. Except that for the first time in his life, he couldn't take care of himself, and, without his paycheck, his assets were diminishing rapidly. He knew he couldn't return to work yet because he wouldn't be able to pass the mandated drug test, and his life was a mess.

Although he'd been raised to say his prayers at night and recite grace at the table, he'd outgrown his need for God (or so he thought). At the same time, however, he illogically blamed God for his situation. "Hey, look what He did to me," he shouted, pounding his chest. To Brandon's way of thinking, he had no reason to love God, and now that he'd been caught in this crisis without any spiritual resources in his life, he didn't know how he'd survive.

Brandon admitted that people didn't understand his ego, and when I went around the room asking the other members of the group what the word *ego* meant to them, the general consensus was that it was thinking more of yourself than you should. I wrote the following on my chalkboard so that everyone could see it:

E—Edging

G—God

O—Out

We edge God out by failing to love Him and express our gratitude for His many kindnesses. We edge God out by failing to acknowledge Him as our Father. As Solomon so wisely told his son, "In all thy ways acknowledge him, and he shall direct thy paths" (Proverbs 3:6). When we replace God the Almighty with our own fallible little selves as the object of our worship, we all eventually come to regret it, for without His mercy and compassion, we are nothing.

As I explained to Brandon, we can't love God if we don't trust Him, and we learn to trust Him by professing our love for Him. Once we give our love to God, we obey His commandments because we trust Him to lead us in the right direction. As is my custom, I then gave him a Bible with selected passages marked and suggested that he read them aloud until he had memorized them.

DAY AFTER DAY, WE DENY HIM

Not only do we place other gods before Him, but more and more we cast Him out of our everyday life. We cast Him out of our schools. Not only have we banished the Lord's Prayer from the classroom, we've removed the words *under* God from the Pledge of Allegiance. And now, I hear, there's a movement to remove the words *in* God *we trust* from our currency.

I understand, of course, the importance of safeguarding the separation of Church and State that guarantees religious freedom for all, but it also seems to me that the more we remove God from our daily lives, the easier it is to edge Him out entirely.

But in the end, when, as our elders used to say, "Where can we go but to the Lord?" we will return to Him, because, as He has proved over and over again, He is alpha and omega.

Marcy and Brandon both learned this lesson the hard way. They thought they knew what was best for them and they didn't want any "big daddy" God figure telling them how to live their lives. In their time of trouble, however, they came to realize that without His wisdom and His guidance, their lives had become runaway trains heading for a major derailment.

DON'T WAIT UNTIL YOUR
HOUR OF NEED

Sometimes we need to be reminded of all that God has done and will continue to do for us if we will only let Him be our guide. That's what He was doing when He said to Moses, "I *am* the Lord thy God, which have brought thee out of the land of Egypt, out of the house of bondage" (Exodus 20:2). He might have prefaced those words by saying, "Hey, have you forgotten who I am?"

For many of us, it's easy to forget about God when times are good and our life is running smoothly—or seems to be. But I would suggest that we make a big mistake when we edge Him out until we have nowhere else to turn. Rather, we'd be much better off keeping Him in our heart and our mind at all times because, by doing that, He'll guide us to avoid the dangers that come from looking to little self-made gods that don't really have any power.

COMMANDING THOUGHTS

- Do you believe God is real?

- Do you acknowledge His presence in your life?

- Are you steadfast in your faith that God deserves first place in your life?

- Are there other gods in your life?

- Put God first in your life.

- Let God be God!

CHAPTER TWO

"THOU SHALT NOT MAKE UNTO THEE ANY GRAVEN IMAGE"

EXODUS 20:4

> *"We easily fall into idolatry, for we are inclined there-*
> *unto by nature, and coming to us by inheritance, it*
> *seems pleasant."*
>
> —MARTIN LUTHER, *Table Talk*

Why would God issue such a command? And why would it apply not only to Him but, as He said, to "any thing that is in heaven above, or that is in the earth beneath, or that is in the water under the earth?" Why? Because if we did that, we would be lured into believing that by worshipping the image we had made we were worshipping God Himself, and we would attribute to the image a power it did not possess.

Much of the dissension in this world has been

31

caused by people who could not agree on how to represent God, and yet we know that each one of us who is descended from Adam is made in His image, because, as Genesis tells us, "In the day that God created man, in the likeness of God made He him." In fact, when I'm conducting a service, I often tell my congregation, "If you want to see God, turn to your left, turn to your right, and say to the person next to you, 'Look at God, because I am made in the image of God.'"

Does that mean He is tall or short, fat or thin, light, dark, brown, yellow, or white? Of course not. It means that the characteristics of God have been deposited in us, and our physical body is simply the house, the vessel, in which God's spirit lives. And so, when we attempt to make an "image" of God we instantly diminish Him, because we have no way of doing that except to represent Him as a physical being rather than a spiritual one.

DON'T DIMINISH THE DIVINE

The problem is that for too many of us, if we can't see it or touch it, we can't believe it exists. It's as if we all came from Missouri—the "show me" state. However, as James Wendell Johnson put it in his poem "The Creation":

> This great God,
> Like a mammy bending over her baby,
> Kneeled down in the dust
> Toiling over a lump of clay
> Till he shaped it in his own image;
> Then into it he blew the breath of life
> And man became a living soul.

But man was actually the last of God's creations. Before He made us, He created the universe in which we live—the mountains, rivers, sky, trees, everything that is on and in the earth God created. And in us He created the mind and the imagination to invent every single thing that came after, from the first most primitive shelter to the latest most advanced technological gadget. And that's why He forbade us to try to make any kind of physical representation of Him or His creation—because by doing that we would automatically be reducing it to something much less than what He had already made. We ourselves are already the greatest of His creations. When we look upon one another, we see not just God's handiwork, but the living representation of the Almighty Himself. King David acknowledged this when he said in Psalm 139, "I will praise thee; for I am fearfully *and* wonderfully made: marvellous *are* thy works; and *that* my soul knoweth right well" (Psalms 139:14).

That's why it's so unbelievable to me that so many people want to "improve" on His creation by embellishing themselves with tattoos. What are tattoos, really, but explicit, visual expressions of the little gods we choose to idolize? It might be a lover's name or some image of virility or even a symbol of death, such as a skull and bones. Those markings then become permanent, although the "idol" that inspired them may be far more fleeting. I remember, for example, visiting an old gentleman in a nursing home. His body was covered with tattoos that had wrinkled as he aged, and when I asked him about the woman's name emblazoned on his arm, he had no recollection of who she was.

I suggest that before we consider such permanent disfigurement, we remember that tattoos were a way for masters to identify their slaves and for Nazi slave-holders to identify their Jewish prisoners. Even in the Bible we learn of the beast of blasphemy that caused his idolatrous worshippers "to receive a mark in their right hand, or in their foreheads" (Revelation 13:16) and are told that "If any man worship the beast and his image, and receive *his* mark in his forehead, or in his hand, The same shall drink of the wine of the wrath of God" (Revelation 14:9–10).

Personally, I don't think the way God created us requires any so-called improvement. Have you ever begun to contemplate the miracle of being able to wink and blink your eyes? Of being able to command your feet to walk without even thinking about it? Of being able to speed up or slow down, hop, skip, or jump at will? Breathe in and breathe out? Go to sleep and wake up? All without conscious effort? How could any one of us possibly improve upon that or encapsulate and represent that kind of power on paper, in clay, or in stone? We can't. And, therefore, if we attempt to make an image of God, and then bow down to or worship that image, we are actually failing to connect directly with the invisible and incomparable power of God.

NO ONE MAN CAN REPRESENT GOD

In the 1950s The Platters had a hit song titled "The Great Pretender," which contained the lyric "I seem to be what I'm not, you see." In the African American culture there have been those who have looked upon one or another of God's ministers, such as Daddy Grace or Father Divine, as His representation on earth. Daddy Grace, who founded the United House of Prayer for all People, attracted an enormous following, and his denomination, which today numbers about 3.5 million worshippers, still flourishes. During his lifetime, Daddy Grace made the godlike prediction that one of his ministers would rise up to take his place after his death, and he also amassed considerable temporal wealth by creating a line of products claimed to have healing powers, including coffee, tea, soaps, and hand creams. Father Divine founded the Peace Movement, the largest religious movement in the northern ghettos during the Depression, and was an early crusader for civil rights, but he was also one of the biggest landlords in Harlem and the owner of restaurants and grocery stores.

There's no doubt that both these men, and many who've come after them, have been devout religious leaders of their flocks, but they were not gods, nor were they endowed with godly powers. There has been only one true representation of God on earth, and that was His son, Jesus.

When we look to any human being for salvation, we diminish God by seeing Him in man's image as opposed to the other way around. By looking to one man for salvation, various denominations have seen God as short and bald, or having a beard, or wearing glasses. But what happened to all these god surrogates? They died, and much as their followers may have waited for them to rise again, they didn't. Only the one true son of God has arisen from death, and he was not resurrected to walk the earth again. No! He was resurrected in spirit and to spirit he returned.

I find it amusing that these "little gods" now surround themselves with security details and bodyguards to protect them from their acolytes. What kind of god would fear those who worship him? Only a false and fallible god who fears being found out.

BEWARE OF WORSHIPPING FAKE GODS

I find it interesting that one of the top-rated television programs in the United States is *American Idol*. Each year America votes to anoint a single performer to idolize. Then the following year that idol is dethroned and another is anointed. While he or she reigns, however, we buy his recordings, read news items about her, and wear items of clothing declaring our "fan"atacism. To each of these transient, pretend gods we create— we offer—a kind of worshipful devotion—until the next one comes along.

And it's also these false gods that we try to emulate. Instead of living in God's image, we spend our lives trying to live up to some image of beauty or power that we have created and that comes and goes with time. What's in fashion today will be out tomorrow. But God never goes out of style.

In our hearts, whether we can see Him or not, we

must know a real God is out there, because He's the one we invariably turn to in times of chaos, crisis, or calamity. Sadly, however, we too often ignore Him except when we're in need. At other times we are more likely to worship the false gods of celebrity, wealth, and glamour. Gods we created. And why do we think we can ignore Him? Because we know in our heart of hearts that He'll be there when we need Him. He won't desert us, even though we may desert Him.

I remember in particular a couple in their mid-forties named Nathan and Angie who apparently considered themselves superior to virtually everyone they knew. They worshipped their own accomplishments and acquisitions, from their fancy car to their fancy home and their fancy wardrobes. Nathan and Angie let it be known that they had no need for religion because "stuff like that" was "a crutch for weak people." "I can take care of myself and Angie," Nathan declared proudly.

And then one day I received a frantic phone call. It was Nathan, and he needed to see me right away. He sounded so distraught that I found the time to see him the very next day. When he arrived, I hardly recognized him. This was no longer the dapper, disdainful man I knew; this man was beaten, bedraggled, and gaunt. Tearfully he explained that Angie had been diagnosed with a particularly virulent form of cancer, and despite everything he had done—taking her from one specialist to the next, providing the best care his money could buy—her condition continued to deteriorate.

Everything had changed overnight, and Nathan was both desolate and angry. When I asked whom he was angry with, he replied, "I'm angry with God." "But you don't believe in God," I reminded him. "How can you be angry with a God you don't believe in?" Chagrined, Nathan admitted that he wanted to pray but didn't know how because he'd never before had the need to pray. Up to that point he'd been able to handle whatever came his way all on his own, but now he was at a loss and he'd heard about the power of prayer. He wanted to learn how to harness that power.

I reminded him of those well known biblical words "Vanity of vanities; all *is* vanity" (Ecclesiastes 1:2), and he admitted that he'd always mocked people who relied on God and acknowledged that he'd been a worshipper at the shrine of materialism. Now, however, he realized that all that was no more than "show and tell." He had learned the hard way the truth of the old saying "money can't buy happiness," and his possessions no longer held any meaning for him. It wasn't until his darkest hour that he realized how false and unworthy his little gods had been and how much he needed to connect with the one true God.

As we continued to talk, I explained to Nathan that his prayers might not change his situation but they would change him, and he agreed that there were many things about him that needed to change. He wanted the presence of a higher power in his life and to reassess his priorities.

Nathan and Angie moved from their multistory home to an apartment that Angie could navigate more easily, and they traded in their Mercedes for an SUV that would accommodate her wheelchair. He and Angie both realized that even though they were living with less, they were able to find an inner piece and a ray of hope.

Angie went through a debilitating course of chemotherapy during which she lost her hair and a lot of weight, but Nathan's response to these trials was, "Hey,

REV. DR. ARLENE CHURN

by the grace of God, she's still here and happy." They found themselves glowing and growing in their new-found spirituality, and when Angie was finally told that her cancer was in remission, she proclaimed, "There is a God and He has answered my prayers."

In the end, I suggested to Nathan that he add the word *blessed* to his vocabulary. The only way to truly worship God is through our obedience and adherence to His commandments. We worship our God through our praise and thanksgiving, and, it has been said, when praises go up, the blessings come down! Many of us, like Nathan, are here to attest to the fact that even when we disobey Him, God will give us a second chance.

IT'S WHAT'S ON THE INSIDE
THAT COUNTS

For Nathan and Angie, image had been everything. Too many of us spend too much of our life worrying about what's on the outside. We think that if we dress up our body and make up our face, if we change the way we look on the outside to project a certain image, people will think better of us. And maybe they will for a while, but eventually they're going to see right through the facade. In fact, you may be fooling yourself more than you're fooling the people you want to fool. And that can wind up getting you in a whole lot of trouble, as one of my clients found out.

Derrick's father brought him to me for counseling because, he said, if Derrick didn't start listening to someone he was going to wind up dead. Twenty-three years old and a high school dropout, Derrick was tall and good looking and tried to pass himself off as savvy and tough. All he wanted to do was manage hip-hop and rap groups, and he seemed to think that he could succeed on looks alone.

When I asked him what he knew about the entertainment industry, his response was, "How much is there to know?" All he knew was that music was "hot" and that, as a manager, he needed to "get bookings, advertise, and sell tickets. How hard can that be? I just need to make the right contacts, get some up-front money, and the money will roll in." Reeking of arrogance, Derrick had constructed a grandiose image of himself and seemed to think that he could convince others as much as he'd convinced himself. He truly believed that if he met the "right" people—that is, people with money and power—they would perceive him to be capable of becoming "the best in the business" and back him all the way.

Much as I tried to convince him at that first meeting that he didn't really know as much as he thought he did, I doubt he heard a word I had to say. I warned him that arrogance and ignorance were a lethal combination, and at that point he just picked up and left.

It was several months before he returned with his father. This time, however, the strut had gone out of his stride and he looked demoralized and defeated. It turned out that in the time since we'd last met Derrick had gotten involved with a couple of guys who turned out to be big-time scam artists. He'd taken them on a tour of his "hood," high-fiving guys along the way and generally putting himself out there as someone with a great deal of "street cred." None of it was true, of course, but the scenario had the dual advantage in Derrick's mind of impressing both the scam artists and the guys on the street. His newfound friends told Derrick it was obvious to them that he was "on the ball" and that they liked "his style." Of course, this was all he needed to hear; because of his arrogance, Derrick was an easy mark.

It didn't take much for them to convince him that because of the fancy clothes he wore and the way he carried himself, he could easily become a big-time drug dealer and make a fortune. All he needed to do was "invest" some money with them to buy the drugs and they would make him a partner. Or, as they put it to him, "The bigger the stash, the more the cash." It seemed to Derrick that his dream was about to come true. Without telling his father, he pawned some of the rifles in his treasured collection and handed over the money to his new business partners, who promptly disappeared with his four thousand dollars, never to be seen or heard from again.

Derrick sheepishly admitted he now understood that the scammers had seen right through him. He thought he was fooling them, but instead they saw him as a "dumb fool." His father was furious, of course, but he was also afraid for his son. "He acts like he's someone he's not, and it's going to ruin him," were his exact words. Derrick, meanwhile, wanted to know, "What's wrong with me?"

I explained that he needed to find a way to feel good enough about himself so that he could allow others to see him for what he really was. It's no good talking the talk unless you can also walk the walk, and if you can't, people will figure that out and use it to their advantage. I didn't have to remind him of what could have happened if his drug deal really had gone through and he'd been caught.

Ultimately, Derrick enrolled in a GED program and was determined to go to a community college as soon as he got his diploma. His new image was going to be "I'm just an average guy trying to make it in this crazy world."

If the image you project doesn't accurately reflect who you are, the people who are attracted to that image are not really being attracted to you. In order to have a true and honest relationship, you must allow yourself to be known. That's just what God was telling us when He forbade us to make graven images. He didn't want to be represented as anything other than what He is.

When God appeared to Moses in the burning bush, and Moses asked what he should tell the Israelites when they asked His name, God said, "I AM THAT I AM . . . Thus shalt thou say unto the children of Israel, I AM hath sent me unto you" (Exodus 3:14). What kind of name is that? What does it mean? It means that God is indescribable. It means that any words we might use to try to describe Him would be inadequate, and, therefore, by extension, we have no way to accurately represent Him. Hence His commandment against making graven images.

THE ONLY WAY TO REPRESENT GOD IS BY LIVING A GODLY LIFE

So how do we represent God on earth? The only way to do that is to reflect His spirit within us in the way we live our life. Instead of idolizing and emulating those little fake gods that we create for ourselves, instead of trying to look and act "hot" or "cool" or "bad," we need to look to Him for guidance and say to people, through word and deed, "I am that I am." "What you see is what you get!" I'm me, and I'm trying to be the best me I can be. I'm trying to act in accordance with the Holy Spirit that lives in me and to act as His representative through the choices I make. That, my friends, is all God asks of us.

COMMANDING THOUGHTS

- Do you love God for who He is or for what He can do for you?

- Are you an idol worshipper?

- Avoid association with idol worshippers, who may influence you to idolize them or their false gods.

- Reflect on your priorities.

- Reclaim your trust and faith in God.

- Learn to worship the true God through appreciation of His handiwork.

- Pray to and communicate with the true God who made you and who loves you.

- Live so that others will see the image of God reflected in your walk and your talk.

CHAPTER THREE

"THOU SHALT NOT TAKE THE NAME OF THE LORD THY GOD IN VAIN"

EXODUS 20:7

The Name of God:
G—Great
O—Omnipotent
D—Divine

We all pretty much take it for granted that this commandment is an admonishment against cursing, but it's really more than that. There are many people who, in the general course of their life, don't even believe in God—or at least the way they live is an indication of nonbelief since they don't act in Godly ways. But then, when something bad happens, or they fall on hard times, they're the first to call out to Him: "Oh, Jesus," "Oh, God," "Jesus Christ," "God

help me," "Oh my God," and so on. What this commandment is telling us is that, when we call upon
God, whether in times of crisis or in adoration, we
need to mean it, we need to be serious about it. God is
not to be called upon frivolously.

THANK GOD IN DEED

How often do we say "thank God" without even thinking about the meaning of those words? We can take
His name in vain just as much when we're thanking or
praising Him as we can when we're cursing or calling
upon Him for help.

How many times have we heard a celebrity rush up
on a stage to accept an award and thank God for his
or her success? And how often do we read about those
same celebrities taking drugs or driving drunk or disrespecting their partner in some way? One rap artist
known for his devotion to Christianity told an inter-
viewer on television that "Jesus is my dawg." I know
that "dawg" is a popular slang term for friend or "bro,"
but I still don't understand why anyone would choose
to refer to the son of God as a dawg. In the popular

vernacular, when you "treat someone like a dog," you're treating them badly, so why would anyone think that comparing the son of God to a dog could possibly be anything other than demeaning? That, too, is what the commandment is telling us: When you speak the name of the Lord, think about how you're using it, and don't use it in vain—in silly, demeaning, or meaningless ways. The best way to truly thank God is through our actions.

BE CAREFUL HOW YOU MAKE A NAME FOR YOURSELF

When you make a name for yourself, you have become so prominent for a particular activity or achievement that your name is recognized by one and all. But making a name for yourself can be a two-edged sword. You might, for example, become known for some outstanding positive achievement and then, with one misstep or misjudgment, become even better known for what you did wrong. We all know plenty of well-known people who've fallen into that trap; I don't need to list them here.

The moral is that once you've succeeded in making a name for yourself, you need to be even more vigilant that you don't take your own name in vain by doing something that demeans everything you've worked so hard to achieve.

ALL NAMES HAVE MEANING

God named Himself Lord God Jehovah and gave Adam the great honor and authority to name every "fowl of the air" and "beast of the field." As it says in Genesis 2:19, "whatsoever Adam called every living creature, that was the name thereof." And before the birth of Christ, an angel appeared to Joseph and told him what to name Mary's son: "And she shall bring forth a son, and thou shalt call his name Jesus: for he shall save his people from their sins" (Matthew 1:21). Then, in Philippians 2:9–10, Paul writes to the believers that, because of Christ's obedience, God "hath highly exalted him, and given him a name which is above every name: That at the name of Jesus every knee should bow."

Names are important. Proverbs 22 tells us that "A

good name is rather to be chosen than great riches" and in times past, we were cautioned against bringing shame or disgrace to the family name. Surnames like Miller, Shoemaker, and Taylor identified our profession and therefore, to some degree, our family history and status in life. Other names, such as O'Malley or Martinez or Moscowitz, are still indicators of our ethnic heritage. In some cultures our last name means, literally, "son or daughter of" our father's first name, so, if we bring shame to that name, we bring shame to his name as well.

In the Catholic faith, children choose a saint's name at their first communion, which then gets added to their given name, assumedly so that they will be inspired to assume the characteristics of the person whose name they have taken.

In times past, we African Americans gave our children names that denoted strength and character, names with history, names associated with contributors to society. We named our daughters after beautiful flowers—Daisy, Rose, or Lily—and after qualities we hoped they would embrace, such as Prudence, Grace, or Faith. We named them carefully and thoughtfully after strong grandmothers, gifted aunts, and women of color who had made a significant contribution to the history and betterment of our people—women like Rosa Parks, Mary McLeod Bethune, Marian Anderson, and Lena Horne. It's interesting, in fact, to note that Oprah Winfrey's name is derived from the Old Testament. Oprah was the sister-in-law of Ruth and the grandmother of King David, but I'm sure there are now many little Oprahs of color who were named after the present-day icon of African American women and who have no knowledge of their name's biblical roots. Bestowing such names on our daughters is a way not only to honor the s/heros of our past but also to inspire those who are named in their honor. There's a good reason why no little girls whom I know of are named Jezebel, while Mary remains popular throughout time. Little boys are similarly named Abraham or Thomas, after American presidents who are heroes to African Americans and who were themselves no doubt named after biblical heroes. And no one whom I know of is named Judas!

In biblical times, men often had descriptors added to their names that identified one from the other by indicating their skills or the earthly role they fulfilled. Thus we have, for example, John the Baptist, a disciple of Jesus, who is not to be confused with John the Revelator, an apostle. Young men are still using descriptors to identify one another, but they are very different from those we find in the Bible. It's beyond my understanding why anyone would prefer being referred to as "Homie" or "Dawg" rather than their rightful name. In times gone by we were often admonished to "live up to our name," but now, it seems, many people are living down to the name they've chosen for themselves or that others have chosen for them.

Instead of names connoting and recalling qualities to be revered, we are giving our children made-up names, names with no meaning, names they sometimes can't even pronounce. And, even worse, I'm told by a friend who teaches elementary school that many children don't even recognize their own official birth name when the role is called because it's never used by their family or friends. Instead they have all kinds of nicknames that may be cute or flattering but just as often are silly or demeaning. It's a slippery slope from there to answering to the even more demeaning names we may be called as adults. "Sticks and stones may break my bones but names will never hurt me" may be a rhyme children use to taunt one another, but, in my experience, name-calling can, indeed, cause pain.

Jamal, a short, overweight sixteen-year-old who looked younger than his age, came to me for counseling after he'd attempted suicide because he could no longer take being teased and made the butt of mean and hateful jokes. Because he refused to fight, he was called a faggot and a sissy and was even accused of "messing around" with little boys. After that, neighborhood parents warned their children to stay away from him.

His mother, who was also overweight, was called names, too, but, unlike her son, she simply "cussed out" the name-callers and went about her business. She thought her son was too soft and she couldn't understand the true depths of his torment.

Almost everyone has encountered a bully sometime in his or her life, but in recent times bullying has gone to such an extreme that it's become a topic of national concern. Jamal was so frightened of being bullied that he dreaded going to school. He was, in his mind, both hopeless and helpless. When he saw the news report of a student about his own age who had finally been so tormented that he went on a shooting spree at his school, Jamal figured he'd be better off dead.

He tried to hang himself from a hook with a rope around his neck in his own bedroom, but luckily his mother, who was home at the time, heard a thud as the chair he'd been standing on tipped over, and ran to see what was wrong. He was rushed to the hospital, unconscious but still alive, and then spent several weeks in a mental facility.

After his release, he became more reclusive than ever until his mother finally sought me out in desperation.

"I'm tired of being called names. I just can't stand it," Jamal said in a halting voice, eyes glued to the floor.

I asked him to speak into a tape recorder all the names that wouldn't offend him, names he'd like to be called. You could almost "hear" the smile in his voice as he recited the names he wished applied to him:

handsome, smart, good guy, cool dude, and—to my surprise—funny. When I asked him about that one he said he knew lots of jokes that would make people laugh, and that he loved to do impersonations of famous people. When I then asked him for an impromptu demonstration, I found out that he really was entertaining. Even his mother had never seen this side of Jamal and was happily surprised by his talent.

We arranged for him to transfer to a different school where he could start over with a clean slate, and I told him that, from then on, he needed to immediately correct anyone who called him anything other than his rightful name. At the same time I suggested that if he managed to lose some weight he would no longer have to worry about being called Fatso and would also be healthier and have more energy. In addition, I shared my own experiences of having been teased because I was fat as a child and wore thick glasses. My revenge was to be the smartest one in the class so that it wasn't long before my tormenters were being called "dumb."

Several years later Jamal has graduated college and become a high school teacher. Today he is vigilant about interceding whenever he sees bullying taking place.

If you consistently call a dog by a particular name, soon enough, the dog will begin to respond to that name. While I'm certainly not comparing any person to a dog, the danger is that if we're called by a name long enough, we may very well begin to take on that identity, which is why we need to claim the good names that are ours by right of birth.

Take Melody Terrell, for example. She is a large, buxom, thirty-six-year-old sales associate for a national chain of discount stores who was recently referred to me for anger-management counseling because her emotional outbursts were becoming so frequent and troublesome that her job was in jeopardy.

It was clear at our very first meeting that Ms. Terrell was not only angry but emotionally wounded, and when I asked her what it was that was making her so mad, she replied matter-of-factly, "Because I have been called everything but my name."

When I urged her to elaborate, she went on to explain that as a child she'd been called "chubby fatback," "Miss Piggy," and even "Jolly Green Giant" because of her size. As she grew older, her first boyfriend called her "Big Momma Big-Tits" and "Miss Five-by-Five." I could see that just recalling these insults was bringing her anger and hurt feelings to the surface all over again. Her voice was edged with barely suppressed fury as she declared that she *despised* being called anything other than her given name and felt that the name-calling she suffered was a way of denying her true identity.

While she was in junior college, she said, she'd actually been happy and had succeeded in losing forty-five pounds. With her weight-loss, however, came a new attitude that actually led to an escalation of the name-calling. Now she was called "Miss Uppity," "Miss Phoney," "Miss Thing," and sometimes just "Bitch." Her then-current boyfriend began referring to her as his "squaw," which she took as an insult to the physical features she'd inherited with her Native American blood. Her street name became "Miss T," the "T" standing for Terrible, and as time passed she began to act out what she was called. She hated being referred to as "T" by her coworkers, and she was just plain tired of fighting to be called by her rightful name.

In counseling I asked her whether she thought she was doing anything to counteract the names she was called, or whether, in fact, by lashing out in anger she was living up to the labels imposed on her by others. I suggested that instead of lashing out, she institute a policy of immediately correcting the name-caller by stating, calmly and decisively, "My name is Melody Terrell." And I explained that by reacting so angrily she was actually encouraging those who got pleasure from teasing her by using the name she hated because they knew it was sure to get a rise out of her. No one has the right to demean us with degrading and de-meaning name-calling, but we also have a responsibil-ity to live up to the name we were given at birth rather than *down* to the one others choose to call us.

"THEY CALL ME MR. TIBBS"

When Sidney Poitier spoke those words it was a declaration that he would not tolerate disrespect. Per-sonally, I remember being admonished as a child ad-dressing an elder to "put a handle on it" as a sign of respect, and I wouldn't have considered calling an adult by his or her first name without a "Miss" or a "Mister" in front of it. Nowadays, however, such verbal niceties tend to fall by the wayside, as does the respect they convey. When we disrespect others, however, we are disrespecting ourselves as well.

Teaching us to address our elders with respect meant that our good manners would reflect well on them. If we were rude or unmannerly, we'd be bringing shame on ourselves and on our parents—on our good name. Which is yet another reason why we must not take the Lord's name in vain. God said He "will not hold him guiltless that taketh his name in vain," but in truth, by doing that, we are already proving ourselves guilty. By disrespecting Him we are acting shamefully, and, therefore, we shame ourselves.

COMMANDING THOUGHTS

- Be mindful of the holiness of God's name.

- Invoke the power of His name in times of plenty as well as in times of trouble.

- Learn the origin and meaning of your name.

• Give your children names that have positive
  meanings.

• Demand respect for your name and respect
  the names of others.

• Celebrate the diversity of names from
  different cultures.

CHAPTER FOUR

"REMEMBER THE SABBATH DAY, TO KEEP IT HOLY"

EXODUS 20:8

"The Law of the Sabbath is the keystone of the arch of public morals; take it away and the whole structure falls."

—ANONYMOUS

God was very careful to make this commandment complete and explicit: "Six days shalt thou labour, and do all thy work: But the seventh day *is* the sabbath of the Lord thy God: *in it* thou shalt not do any work, thou, nor thy son, nor thy daughter, thy manservant, nor thy maidservant, nor thy cattle, nor thy stranger that *is* within thy gates" (Exodus 20:9–10).

Years ago, the seventh day—whether you call it the

Sabbath or the Lord's Day—was truly a day to rest and to honor God and His Creation. Stores were closed, professional sports teams didn't play. No one went to the mall or to the movies. Many states even passed "blue laws" prohibiting merchants from doing business and liquor from being sold on the Sabbath. In my home, the television remained off until after sunset— just in time for my grandmother to see *The Ed Sullivan Show*, which she loved. I remember those days with great fondness. They were days filled with food, family, fellowship, and worship. Every child had a Sunday outfit—little patent leather shoes for the girls and a black or navy suit with a white shirt and a clip-on bow tie for the boys. Women were decked out in their most fabulous hats with gloves and a purse dangling from their wrist. The men were in suits with a starched white shirt and a plain dark necktie. When you saw a family dressed in their finery, you knew where they were going. You knew they were obeying God's commandment to "keep it holy."

ON WHICH DAY DID HE REST?

After all the work God did creating every living thing, He looked upon what He had done, He declared it good, and He rested. We now accept the fact that a biblical "day" may not have consisted of the same twenty-four-hour period by which we measure our days. But however long it took Him to complete His creation, when it was done God took the time to rest and bless what He had accomplished.

In pre-Christian times the Sabbath was celebrated on Saturday, the last day of the week. Biblical scholars still argue about when and why the Christian Sabbath began to be celebrated on Sunday, but one generally accepted reason is that Christ was resurrected on Sunday. We know this because we are told in Mark 16 that "when the Sabbath [which was then Saturday] was past, Mary Magdalene, and Mary the *mother* of James, and Salome, had bought sweet spices, that they might come and anoint him. And very early in the morning the first *day* of the week [i.e., Sunday], they came unto the sepulchre at the rising of the sun. . . . And entering into the sepulchre, they saw a young man sitting on the right side, clothed in a long white garment; and they were affrighted. And he saith unto them, Be not affrighted: Ye seek Jesus of Nazareth, which was crucified: he is risen; he is not here" (Mark 16:1–2, 5–6). In addition, changing the Lord's day was a way for the Church of Rome to differentiate itself from Judaism. The Emperor Constantine made the change "official" in the fourth century AD at the Council of Nicea. And Jews, of course, still keep the Sabbath from sundown on Friday until sundown on Saturday.

Whatever the day, however, God tells us that when His work was done He rested. I have no doubt that He could have gone on to create something else. I have no clue what that might have been, but I'm sure it, too, would have been "good." However, God (unlike many of us) knew when to quit; He knew when enough was enough. He took the time to enjoy and pay honor to the work he had done, and He's telling us that we need to do the same. In other words, He's asking us both to rest and to pay honor to Him and His work. As He said to Moses on the mountain, "Speak thou also unto the children of Israel, saying, Verily my sabbaths ye shall keep: for it *is* a sign between me and you throughout your generations; that *ye* may know that I *am* the Lord that doth sanctify you" (Exodus 31:13).

God wants us to show our love for Him as He shows His for us. We know that he loves us because, as it says in Lamentations 3:22–23, "*It is of* the Lord's mercies that we are not consumed, because his compassions fail not. *They are* new every morning."

TAKE A PAGE FROM HIS BOOK

We miss out on a lot when we don't observe the Sabbath. I call it taking "a rest from the test." I don't know what your weeks are like, but if they're anything like mine, from Monday through Saturday it's hectic, exhausting, and frustrating. So God knew that after those six challenging days, we needed a mental, spiritual, physical, and emotional day of rest. God blessed that day and made it holy, and we need to position ourselves to be in the path of those blessings. But how do we do that? Well, we don't do it by staying in bed all day. God didn't call it "a day of sleep." We do it by resting in the presence of the Lord, which means not only going to a place of worship but also doing things we enjoy in a celebratory state of obedience to God.

God knows us very well—after all, He created us. And He knows that, as it states in Isaiah 30:15, "In returning and rest shall ye be saved; in quietness and in confidence shall be your strength." And then again, in Isaiah 40:29–31, we are told, "He giveth power to the faint; and to *them that have* no might he increaseth strength. Even the youths shall faint and be weary, and the young men shall utterly fall: But they that wait upon the Lord shall renew *their* strength; they shall mount up with wings as eagles; they shall run, and not be weary; *and* they shall walk, and not faint." And He prevailed upon us in Psalms 46:10 to "Be still, and know that I *am* God" because, by doing that, we will soar like eagles.

Every thing and every day that He created, He declared "good," and we need to make the seventh day a good day. We have many different kinds of days—long days, crazy days, hard days—but how often can we really say we've had a good day? "Have a good day" is a commonly used phrase for politely ending a conversation, but it was the Lord Himself who initially admonished us to have at least one good day a week, one day that we set aside as hallowed and holy, a day to spend in His presence. Can't you do that? He asks. Can't you spend just one day with me? Is there not one day that you can set aside for me?

By asking us to do this, God also reminds us that we are free and able to refrain from work at least one day a week. When Moses is reiterating the Ten Commandments to the children of Israel in Deuteronomy 5:15 he states, "And remember that thou wast a servant in the land of Egypt, and *that* the Lord thy God brought thee out thence through a mighty hand and by a stretched out arm: therefore the Lord thy God commanded thee to keep the sabbath day." With these words he is reminding the Israelites that they were slaves in Egypt, and slaves didn't get to take a day off. To this day, part of the purpose of the Jewish Sabbath is to remember the Exodus and the gift of freedom God gave His people.

Not too long ago I was leading a weekend retreat for women. One of the attendees—I'll call her Alma—was completely burned out from following a daily routine that would have killed a workhorse. She got up every morning at 4:30 in order to get her grand-children ready for school and then stop by her ailing mother's house to check on her and administer her medicine, all before arriving at work by 7:45. After work, she picked up the grandchildren, again checked on her mother, and then went home to make dinner, wash up, do the laundry, help the "grands" with their homework and get them to bed, and then try to get to bed herself by 11:30.

Alma told me that she loved church, but she was just too tired on Sunday to do anything or go any-where. And, in any case, just because it was Sunday didn't mean that she got to take the day off from car-ing for her mother. She'd come on the retreat at the insistence of a friend who was afraid she was on the verge of a complete breakdown.

I suggested to Alma—and all the other women on the retreat who were trying to find a better way of life—that mama birds sit on their eggs without mov-ing for as long as it takes for them to hatch, and that like the birds, they, too, needed to rest and nest in the Lord—rest in His presence at church and then return home to do some spiritual nesting.

HE BLESSED YOU TO BLESS HIM

So, asking us to refrain from work and spend a day with Him is yet another gift God gives us. During the week the pendulum of our life swings from one extreme to the other. I'm sure you've heard the expression "running late." You've probably used it yourself a few times in the past week. It seems as if we're always behind time, and then we spend time trying to make up for the time we've lost. Despite all the so-called time-saving devices we've come up with—from no-iron sheets to dishwashers, microwaves, and George Foreman grills, we still don't have enough time.

What's happened to all that time we're saving? In days past, there were homemade rolls hot out of the oven on Sunday morning. We sat around the breakfast table, prayed, and each child was required to recite a Bible verse. (The shortest verse in the Bible, "Jesus wept," was not acceptable.) The meal was prepared, eaten, and the dishes washed by hand—all before Sunday school began at 9:30. Families worshipped together and afterward sat down together to Sunday dinner. We ate in the dining room—no television, no radio—and talked. We caught up on what each family member had been doing that week, and in the course of those family meals we children also learned manners. And then we all returned to church for the afternoon service. In the evening, neighbors might stop by for dessert and a chat. The day of rest was a day of bonding during which we learned how to communicate with one another and acknowledge our blessings.

We need to recapture those days before we wind up working ourselves to death, which is what Gerald, a forty-two-year-old father of six children ages four, seven, nine, thirteen, fifteen, and sixteen, was well on the way to doing when I met him. Our first meeting was in jail, where Gerald was waiting for his brother to bail him out after he'd gotten into a physical fight with one of his coworkers. He looked broken and exhausted, and he told me ruefully that his night behind bars was "the best sleep I've had in ages." Gerald had been working two full-time jobs for eight years, and in the evenings and on weekends he also worked for a moving company. When I asked him what he and his family did for recreation, his answer was, "You're kidding!"

When he got out of jail and came to see me for counseling, it was clear that Gerald was on the brink of exploding. He'd lost one of his two jobs and was finding it harder than ever to make ends meet. He was worn out, tired, drained, and saw no way out of his miserable situation. Much as he loved his family, trying to provide all the things they wanted—which for the kids meant expensive sneakers, video games, tickets to rap concerts, and cell phones—was killing him. He also bemoaned the fact that the children weren't doing as well as they should in school, his wife couldn't really control them, and because he was working all the time, he wasn't around to see that they did their homework.

I asked him when he had last attended church with his family, and he just shook his head. Although they'd been to a few funerals, he couldn't remember their actually attending a service. He'd grown up in the church, but his wife wasn't interested in going, so church attendance had just sort of fallen by the wayside, and now his kids had no interest either. I suggested that he read not only the commandment to observe the Sabbath but also Joshua 24:15, which states, "But as for me and my house, we will serve the Lord," and that he seek guidance from Psalms 121 ("My help cometh from the Lord, which made heaven and earth") and 122 ("I was glad when they said unto me, Let us go into the house of the Lord").

People come up with many reasons for not going into the house of the Lord. I believe I've heard them all: The service is too long; the preacher is too loud; they ask for too much money; it's the only day I have to sleep late; I don't have any proper church clothes; I don't have to go to church to serve the Lord. But God didn't give us options; He saw and thought of everything, including how and where we are expected to honor Him.

Like so many of us, Gerald needed to get his priorities straight. His having lost one of his jobs meant that the family had to make some sacrifices, but it also meant that Gerald had more time to spend with them. I suggested that just because he was big and strong didn't mean he was acting big and strong, and I recommended that he call a family meeting at which he would be the keynote speaker and assert that from then on his household was going to be operating with some new rules and regulations. I reminded him that while Moses was away on the mountain communing with the Lord, the children of Israel lost their way, and God sent Moses back down to "straighten them out," saying, "Go, get thee down; for thy people, which thou broughtest out of the land of Egypt, have corrupted *themselves*" (Exodus 32:7), and I suggested that his own children could also use some straightening out. Later, we both laughed when he described having to virtually drag the kids to church, but he got them there, and after a while they, too, became more involved and even joined the youth choir.

Gerald also found support and friendship among the men in the congregation, and ultimately he and another church member bought themselves a truck and started a lucrative moving business of their own. Both he and his wife were thrilled with his new success but pledged that—tempting as it might be—there would be no more working on Sundays. Now he freely admits that since they began going to church, he and his family have grown spiritually and are closer and happier than ever before. Gerald says they've been blessed beyond their expectations.

APPRECIATE HIS GIFT

Every day we go forth and do battle against the negative forces out there that wear us down and wear us out, and we need the Sabbath to replenish our spiritual tools so that we can once more face the world renewed and refreshed.

We need to appreciate God's having given us this day of rest. We should appreciate the fact that He knew we would be mentally and physically challenged every day and that we needed not only His permission but His actual command to take a day off and become reenergized. On this day we need to take the advice of an old Negro hymn and "just steal away." Remember, this is the day the Lord hath made. Rejoice and be glad in it.

COMMANDING THOUGHTS

- What do you do with the six days God gave you for yourself?

- What is your justification for not worshipping and resting on the Sabbath?

• Do you confuse sleeping with resting?

• Are you willing to try using the Lord's Day as a "stress eliminator"? It works.

• Do you see that God wants more for you than you want for yourself?

• Can you try doing things His way?

• Can you set this day aside for your spiritual growth?

CHAPTER FIVE

"HONOUR THY FATHER AND THY MOTHER"

EXODUS 20:12

"I think it must somewhere be written that the virtues of mothers shall be visited on their children, as well as the sins of their fathers."

—CHARLES DICKENS

God Himself is our heavenly Father; when we pray it is to "Our father which art in heaven." For Roman Catholics, the pope is known as the Holy Father because he is the representation of Christ on earth. And among nuns, the highest ranking in any order is known as the Mother Superior. These are honorary titles, intended to convey respect for those who are closest to the Lord.

As we honor Him, God also asks us to honor our

earthly fathers and mothers, just as we would want our children to honor us. It's interesting that following this commandment God says, "That thy days may be long upon the land which the Lord thy God giveth thee." To me this is a reminder that we will some day be in the position our parents are now in and that our roles with relation to our own children will be reversed. In fact, a good friend of mine who is now caring for her mother says, "When people ask me if I have any children, I say, 'Oh, yes, I have one. She's eighty-three years old.'"

To honor is to respect, revere, appreciate, and be grateful for. All of those aspects of honor God asks us to show our parents. In Exodus 21:17 He tells us that "he that curseth his father, or his mother, shall surely be put to death." And yet, too many children seem to think that whatever their parents do for them or give to them is theirs by right of birth and that they also have the right to cuss and make outrageous demands on them at will.

I think of my dear friend who loved her son unconditionally and indulged his every whim. She denied him nothing, but as the years went on his demands became more and more outrageous—he demanded not only her time but also her money and the use of her car. If she made any attempt to object, he berated and chastised her as if she were a servant rather than a parent.

For a long time the young man's father sat silently by, until he could no longer stand for his wife's being treated that way and finally spoke up. "Son," he said, "I've been listening to how you speak to your mother. All that whooping and hollering, all the disrespect. If your mother wants to take it, that's between you and her, but your mother also happens to be my wife, and I will not tolerate your disrespecting my wife. The next time I hear you disrespecting my wife, you're out of this house."

The boy was stunned. He couldn't believe it, but he could tell from the expression on his father's face that he meant every word. From that moment on he changed his attitude toward his mother.

If we want respect and honor from our children, we must show them that we respect and honor each other, because that is the honorable thing to do. Mothers and fathers both need to lead by example, to show their children through their behavior how they are expected to behave. If parents don't act respectfully and lovingly to each other, how can they expect their children to be loving and respectful of them—or of anyone else for that matter?

TO BE HONORED WE MUST BE HONORABLE

Jesus honored his father, and God, in turn, honored His son by saying, in Matthew 3:17, "This is my beloved Son, in whom I am well pleased." Honor, in other words, is a mutual obligation.

I'm horrified these days when I hear about children who have no time for their aging parents, who actually appropriate their parents' assets without their knowledge, and who place parents in institutions so that they won't be a "burden" to them. But I'm also distressed by how some parents are raising their children and what children are exposed to because of parents' behavior.

Of course, bad parenting is nothing new. Even in biblical times, there were less than honorable parents.

Take, for example, Rebecca, wife of Isaac, mother of Esau and Jacob. When Isaac was old and could not see, he called his eldest son, Esau, to him and bade him bring venison for a feast, that Isaac might bless him before he died. But Rebecca overheard their conversation and sent her younger son, Jacob, to impersonate his brother so that Isaac might bless him instead (Genesis 27).

And then there was Herodias, whom King Herod took as his wife even though John the Baptist told him it was wrong because she had been married to Herod's brother. When Herodias sent her daughter to dance for Herod, he was so enchanted that he promised the girl half his kingdom plus whatever else she asked of him. When she then asked her mother what she should request, Herodias told her to ask for the head of John the Baptist. And even though Herod was very upset because he knew that John was a good and honorable man, he could not go back on his promise (Mark 6:18–26).

So even in the Bible there are parents who lead their children astray, but there are also those leaders who provide wise guidelines for parents. In Proverbs

31:2–9 King Lemuel repeats the litany of proper behavior taught him by his mother, and in Proverbs 22:6, King Solomon advises us to "train up a child in the way he should go: and when he is old, he will not depart from it." One of the ways we do that is to teach our children to respect the elders of the community because, in that way, we are also teaching them to respect us.

One young man who was "trained up" right had moved from his hometown to another city where he became involved in a relationship with a special young lady. The first time his parents came to visit him in his new home, he let the young lady know that she'd have to stay at her own place that night. Since she lived some distance away and was accustomed to spending several nights a week with him, she was surprised by his decision. "I can't let my mom and dad see me sleeping with anyone I'm not married to," he explained. Again, because he was so independent and certainly "of age," she expressed her surprise. "You don't know my parents," he said. "That's the way I was brought up." Notice that he didn't say *he* thought it was wrong of them to be sleeping together; he was simply honoring what he knew to be his parents' feelings about the matter.

I hear many parents today saying, "I want to be my child's friend" or, "I'm not going to be as strict with my children as my parents were with me." While we certainly want to act in ways that will encourage our children to like and admire us rather than fear us, we don't do that by being their buddy or pal. We do that by being good parents and good people. We do that by "training them up," not by letting them run wild.

When they do run wild, however, it seems that their parents blame everyone and everything except themselves or their children. Too many parents who, a generation ago, would have been working overtime to provide college tuition are now working overtime to provide bail money—and still they claim, "He's really a good boy. He just got in with the wrong crowd." Surely parents can't and shouldn't be responsible for everything their children do, either good or bad, but they do need to take responsibility for what they do or don't teach them and for exerting as much of a positive influence as they can.

Today we see many mothers who are barely out of

childhood themselves and who want their children to call them by their first names. Even grandmothers protest that "he better not call me grandma. I'm too young to be a grandmother!" and make up nicknames for their grandchildren to call them instead.

Mother, Mommy, Mama, Grandma, Grandpa, Daddy, Father—these are all titles of honor. Using these titles instills in our children an awareness of the respect and honor due to the one who bears the title, just as using the title Mister or Miss or Sir or General does. And using these titles also goes back to God's third commandment, which reminds us of the importance of names.

TO BE HONORED WE MUST
BE RESPONSIBLE

Traditionally, a father's role was to provide for, protect, and train his children, to be involved in their lives. A mother's role was to do the same. And both parents were also expected to be loving, patient, and supportive—to each other as well as to their children. Those are our roles as parents.

Becoming a parent is a big responsibility. Procreation doesn't make us parents. Parenting makes us parents, and sometimes that means putting our children first, even making sacrifices to provide for them. And yet, how often do we see families with big houses, big cars, who haven't done anything to provide for their children's education? How often do we see parents decked out in expensive clothes and jewelry while their children run around looking like ragamuffins?

Or, a father may desert his family entirely, leaving his children and their mother to fend for themselves as best they can. Worse yet, we have children living with foster parents because both their biological parents have been declared unfit, meaning that they have acted irresponsibly and neglected or abused their children, or both. I've attended countless meetings and conferences whose focus was on providing programs and services for children. But the sad fact is that without parental cooperation, no program or service will succeed. These days, many parents don't attend PTA meetings or involve themselves in school functions and more often than not they blame rather than applaud teachers who discipline (or attempt to discipline) their children. In truth, with so many teenagers dropping out of school and becoming parents, these children-having-children simply don't have the education to assist in the education of their own kids. With the National Crime Prevention Council reporting that approximately 1.5 to 2 million children have at least one parent in prison, it's no wonder we're asking "What's the matter with kids today?" The real question ought to be "What's the matter with parents today?"

This is not the scenario God envisioned when He admonished us to honor our fathers and mothers. In truth, I have heard many young people tell me, "I don't respect my mother or my father because they don't respect themselves."

Foster parents are paid to take care of someone else's children, and while many of them are certainly loving and supportive of the children in their care, very often the children—who may go from one foster home to another—are left feeling unloved, untethered, and with no sense of respect for parents in general because of the way they've been raised.

In the African American community it is very often a relative who steps up to raise their grandchildren or nieces and nephews when parents can't or won't. They take on the role of loving parents and become responsible for the children's teaching and care. In consequence, we often hear young people saying, "My grandma raised me. She's more like a mother to me than my own mother." I would like to suggest that it's the duty of the older mothers (and grandmothers) in the community to teach the younger generation how to live with dignity and be worthy of their children's love, honor, and respect.

In the old days godparents also played important roles in the lives of their godchildren. Originally, godparents acted as the baby's sponsors at baptism and were thereafter involved in his or her religious education. Similarly, in the Jewish religion there is a tradition of asking a close friend or relative to ceremonially hold the male baby during circumcision (which is also the occasion of naming the child) or the girl baby during her naming ceremony. Usually, that person will then have some continuing role in the child's life and may even be legally designated his or her guardian should anything happen to the parents.

These days, however, godparents are generally much less involved in the lives of their godchildren, and are too often seen merely as "present givers." It would be wise for parents to consider more carefully whom they ask to be their child's godparents, and to be certain that they are people who will have an ongoing strong and positive influence on the child's upbringing.

Hillary Rodham Clinton breathed new life into the old saying, "It takes a village to raise a child." Today, however, the so-called village is very often the culprit when children go astray. These days people seldom know their neighbors, and many communities are overrun—if not actually run—by drug dealers, gang members, and assorted hustlers. So when responsible and loving elders or godparents do step in to take parental responsibility, they deserve all the honor we can give them, not only as surrogate parents but as elders and preservers of the community itself.

HONOR BY LEARNING TO FORGIVE

Up to this point I've been stressing the need for parents to act honorably and deserving of the honor we give them, but it's also true that God didn't say in His commandment that some parents were more deserving of honor than others. If for no other reason, we can and should honor our parents for having given us life and with it the opportunity—if necessary—to make better choices for ourselves than they did.

Many years ago, I counseled a young man named Herman, who was one of three children who had been abandoned by their father when Herman was eight years old. After his father left, Herman watched as his mother drowned herself in alcohol until she died when he was thirteen. At that point the siblings were separated, each one going to live with a different relative. Unfortunately, Herman's life did not improve. The aunt who took him in let him know that she considered him more a burden than a blessing and continuously reminded him that his father was no good and his mother had drunk herself to death.

Still, Herman graduated in the top 5 percent of his

high school class, won a scholarship to college, went on to earn a master's degree, and joined the FBI. The one thing that continued to plague him, however, was not knowing his father. He wanted to meet him, and, using his professional resources, he finally tracked him down to the nursing home where he was living.

Herman decided not to contact his father in advance for fear that he wouldn't want him to come, and he asked me to accompany him on his first visit. It was a forty-mile drive, and I could tell that Herman was extremely nervous. I assured him that, whatever choices he had made in the past, this man was still his father, and I shared with him the thought that even what seems to us terrible and damaging can bring about something positive and good. In fact, I pointed out, there was no way to know whether he would have achieved as much success in his life if his father hadn't left.

We found Herman's father in the day room, a double amputee confined to a wheelchair. I couldn't believe how much they looked alike. His father must have noticed it, too, because he looked up at Herman and said, "Are you my son?"

"Yes," Herman answered with tears in his eyes. "I'm Herman Jr."

His father closed his eyes then, as if he were in a courtroom awaiting a verdict he feared would be bad, and finally Herman said, "I don't know why I'm here, but I wanted to see you, and I wanted you to see me— to see that in spite of everything I have made something of myself. I think I wanted to say I hate you, but after seeing you, I don't hate you. To do that I would have to hate the you in me, and I happen to like myself."

The old man dropped his head as tears rolled down his cheeks, and then Herman bent down, crying as well, to embrace him. He told his father that when he was a boy he used to lie in bed at night and wish he had a father to hug him just once.

As a nurse approached, the father asked if he could tell her this was his son, and Herman actually blushed as he gave his permission. We left with Herman promising to return very soon, and as we sat in the car laughing and crying, I told him that I knew the meeting had been difficult but that he'd done the right thing. "It felt right," he said, nodding in agreement.

Since then he's kept his promise and has visited many times, saying that for the first time in his life he's understood that honoring his father means showing appreciation simply for having been given the gift of life.

GOD IS GENDER NEUTRAL

In Genesis 1:27–28 we learn that "God created man in his *own* image, in the image of God created he him; male and female created he them. And God blessed them, and God said unto them, Be fruitful, and multiply." In other words, God made both man and woman in His own image, and He gave them equal responsibility for creating new life and for parenting, and He commands us to honor mothers and fathers equally.

In fact, for those of the Jewish religion, God has a specifically feminine aspect that is given a specific name. In the Talmud, which contains the writings of ancient Hebrew scholars elucidating and explaining the Torah (the first five books of the Bible), this feminine aspect is referred to as *Shekinah*, a feminine Hebrew noun meaning the aspect of God that rests among the people and that is looked upon as the compassionate aspect of God.

So God may be looked upon as the first advocate for women's equality. But if mothers and fathers deserve to be honored equally, that means they also have equal responsibility for acting honorably. He is telling us, in this commandment, that by honoring our parents we are honoring His representatives on earth.

In fact, men and women, young and old, parents and children—we all honor God by honoring ourselves and one another, by living in obedience to *all* His commandments. By doing that we are bestowing honor where honor is due.

COMMANDING THOUGHTS

- Do you recognize God as your heavenly Father?

- Do you obey His commandments?

- Do you show respect to your parents?

- Do you honor the elders in your life and community?

- Do you influence young parents to be responsible?

- Whether or not you are a parent, you can have a motherly or fatherly influence on others.

- Remember that God is both your father and your friend.

- Rejoice in your status as a child of God.

CHAPTER SIX

"THOU SHALT NOT KILL"

EXODUS 20:13

*"If we became students of Malcolm X, we would not
have young black men out there killing each other
like they're killing each other now."*

—SPIKE LEE

H ave you ever noticed how many of our modern
euphemisms put a positive twist on the notion
of killing? When we call someone a "ladykiller" we're
implying that he's so debonair, charismatic, and physically attractive that he can seduce any woman he
wants. When a woman has "killer good looks," she's
"drop dead gorgeous." When we hear a particularly
funny joke or story, we're likely to say, "Oh, stop!
You're killing me!" And when someone does something that really annoys us we might say, "Lord, I

could have killed him." But for our Lord, killing isn't, and never has been, a laughing matter, because when we take a life, we're destroying a part of His creation.

The first mention we have in the Bible of a killing occurs almost immediately after Adam and Eve are cast out of the Garden of Eden and Eve gives birth to two sons, Cain and Abel. When the brothers bring their sacrifices to God, He accepts Abel's but rejects Cain's; Cain then becomes angry and kills his brother, apparently in a fit of jealous rage.

Initially, when God questions him about Abel's whereabouts, Cain lies, saying that he doesn't know and asking in mock innocence, "Am I my brother's keeper?" But, of course, God knows all; you cannot lie to the Lord. The result is yet another casting out, for God punishes Cain by telling him that he will be "cursed from the earth," which will not yield crops for him, and that he will be "a fugitive and a vagabond" for the rest of his life. Cain is devastated, not only because he is being cast out but because he fears that "every one that findeth me shall slay me."

But God lets him know that this won't happen because "whosoever slayeth Cain, vengeance shall be taken on him sevenfold," and he places a mark on Cain's forehead so that no one will kill him by mistake (Genesis 4:1–15). However, the mark, it should be noted, also makes it clear to one and all that Cain is a killer.

God knows the horrors attendant upon the killing of a fellow human being, and even though Cain loses His favor, the Lord makes sure that the killings do not continue. In His eyes there is no such thing as "sweet revenge."

And Moses also knew the terrible consequences of killing. While he was in Egypt, Moses killed an Egyptian whom he'd seen beating one of his fellow Hebrews. But even then he knew it was wrong. We know this because the Bible tells us that "he looked this way and that way," and only when he thought no one was watching did he dare to kill, after which he hid the body. It turned out, however, that two of the Hebrew slaves had witnessed the crime, and, even though he had been protecting one of their own, they told Moses that what he'd done was wrong. At that point Moses was afraid—quite rightly as it turned out—that the Pharaoh would find out about the murder and seek revenge. So Moses fled from Egypt and lived in the desert for many years, until God sent him back to rescue the Israelites from bondage (Exodus 2:11–25).

Even the great king David was guilty of murder when he sent Uriah, the husband of his lover, Bathsheba, to the front lines of battle where he was certain to be killed, in order to get him out of the way (2 Samuel 11:14–17). But the Lord was displeased and sent Nathan to deliver this message to David: "Behold, I will raise up evil against thee out of thine own house, and I will take thy wives before thine eyes, and give *them* unto thy neighbour, and he shall lie with thy wives in the sight of this sun. For thou didst *it* secretly: but I will do this thing before all Israel, and before the sun. And David said unto Nathan, I have sinned against the Lord. And Nathan said unto David, The Lord also hath put away thy sin; thou shalt not die. Howbeit, because by this deed thou hast given great occasion to the enemies of the Lord to blaspheme, the child also *that is* born unto thee shall surely die" (2 Samuel 12:11–14).

Many years later, when David was old, he called another son, Solomon, to him and said, "My son, as for me, it was in my mind to build an house unto the name of the Lord my God: But the word of the Lord came to me, saying, Thou hast shed blood abundantly, and hast made great wars: thou shalt not build an house unto my name, because thou hast shed much blood upon the earth in my sight. Behold, a son shall be born to thee, who shall be a man of rest; and I will give him rest from all his enemies round about: for his name shall be Solomon, and I will give peace and quietness unto Israel in his days. He shall build an house for my name; and he shall be my son, and I *will be* his father; and I will establish the throne of his kingdom over Israel for ever. Now, my son, the Lord be with thee; and prosper thou, and build the house of the Lord thy God, as he hath said of thee" (1 Chronicles 22:7–11).

Despite so much incontrovertible evidence that killing is always a sin in the eyes of the Lord, we continue to hear and read day after day of one murder after another. The killer always seems to have a reason—revenge for some real or imagined wrong, jealousy, because the victim "deserved" to die—but there is never a reason to justify taking a life. God didn't say thou shalt not kill *except* in this or that specific circumstance. There weren't any loopholes in His commandment.

These days we talk a lot about "senseless killings." Into this category we certainly place the unprovoked and random mass shootings at Columbine and Virginia Tech or any murder of a stranger for no apparent reason. My question then is, Why do we think it's more senseless to kill a stranger than someone we're close to or even a member of our own family? In most instances, no matter how absurd it may appear to us, the killer is able to come up with some kind of reason for his (or her) act. But again, for God, every killing is ultimately senseless.

Since God, unlike we humans, has the ability to see into the future, He knew the inevitable trickle-down effect of taking a life. We see those consequences today not only when the media interviews the devastated loved ones of the person who has died but also when, for example, gangs wreak revenge on one another. For one gang member murdered, several others often pay with their lives. Still, the problem, whatever it was, isn't solved, and very often innocent bystanders also become victims of the unholy mayhem. In war, this is euphemistically called "collateral damage," as if those who are not the direct targets of the killing don't even count. But they do count in the eyes of God, because we are all His children and we are all made in His image.

FOR GOD THERE ARE NO EXCUSES

How often have we heard a killer claiming that he or she "didn't mean it" or "didn't want him (or her) to die?" Well, if you didn't mean it, why did you do it? Why were you waving a gun around? What were you thinking? We need to remember that when you play with fire, someone is likely to get burned.

Most often, however, the excuse is that the killing was in some way justified. Either the victim "had it coming" because of something he or she did—or that the killer *thought* he or she did—or the killer believed that his own life was in danger. The law does allow for "justifiable homicide," but God's law was made in order to create a world where there was no need for self-protection because *everyone* lived by His word and, therefore, there was no killing.

Clearly we're a long way from achieving such universal détente, but when we're wondering *why* God set down such specific and arbitrary rules for His people, it would be wise of us to consider how different the world would be if we all actually lived by those rules.

I'm sure that we've all, at one time or another—particularly when we hear of a life cut short by a brutal crime—thought that the killer "deserved" to die. In fact, one of the greatest continuing controversies with regard to the law is whether or not there ought to be a death penalty. But as Jesus warned those who came to arrest him at Gethsemane, "All they that take the sword shall perish with the sword" (Matthew 26:52).

In some instances that death may be actual, but in others the killer, who spends the rest of his life in prison, may become one of the "living dead." For many years I counseled a group of convicted murderers who were serving life sentences, and, as one who had murdered his girlfriend put it to me, "For her dying was quick and easy, but for me living is hell."

Among the inmates I visited was Aaron, the product of a broken home and one of eight siblings, none of whom had any relationship with their father. He already had a long juvenile record when he killed a police officer in the course of a liquor store robbery, and when I met him he'd already spent twenty-six of his forty-seven years behind bars. For a long time Aaron claimed that he had no regrets about his crime because, as he said, "The cop would have killed me." As the years went on, however, his attitude began to change, until, in one counseling session, he wept for the first time ever and remorsefully admitted that, although he had been spared the death penalty, he was not really living. Not only was he confined to prison but he was told what to eat and what to wear, and he hadn't even had the simple luxury of taking a bath rather than a quick shower twice a week in all the time he had been there. Moreover, he was completely cut off from his family, who had stopped visiting many years before. For him, too, life was a living hell.

OUR LAW VERSUS GOD'S LAW

Our laws make distinctions among different degrees of killing—first degree murder, second degree murder, and manslaughter. Then there's the question of what kind of murder deserves punishment by death. All of these seem to imply that some killings are worse than others. Is it better to shoot someone than to stab him or poison her? And what about causing death by sheer neglect? God's commandment, as I've said, is clear: "Thou shalt not kill," and that means anyone, under any circumstances. We don't live in a perfect world, and clearly not everyone lives by God's rules, but there can be no doubt that this is something to strive for, because if we did, there would be no need for us to create human laws to compensate for our human shortcomings.

God was, in fact, the first lawgiver and remains our ultimate judge: "For the Lord *is* our judge, the Lord *is* our lawgiver" (Isaiah 33:22). As citizens we all abide by thousands of laws every day, laws that impact our homes, our vehicles, our utilities, our children, our food, medicine, and even our recreation. But if we stop to think about it—upon what are all those laws based? Ultimately, they are designed to ensure that we live by the laws of God. As King David so wisely put it: "The law of the Lord *is* perfect, converting the soul:

the testimony of the Lord *is* sure, making wise the simple. The statutes of the Lord *are* right, rejoicing the heart: the commandment of the Lord *is* pure, enlightening the eyes" (Psalms 19:7–8).

The Lord, therefore, reserves unto Himself the right to pass judgment on our sins. His judgments may not always seem logical to us because we don't know as much as He does. But when we take that right into our own hands and act as His executioners, we are, in fact, setting ourselves up as false little gods, because we do not have the wisdom to make such life or death decisions.

SAY NO TO KILLERS OF THE SPIRIT

When we speak about murder, the prohibition seems perfectly clear. No one has the right to take another person's life. But what about killing the spirit? Is that not also destroying a life? We've all heard people called killjoys—those who seem to take pleasure in sucking the pleasure out of other people's lives. This too is a kind of murder because it causes—or attempts to cause—a death of the spiritual joy that connects us to the power and glory of the Lord and gives us confidence in ourselves. No one has the right to do that to another human being. If someone tries to kill your joy, you must remember that "The joy of the Lord is your strength" (Nehemiah 8:10).

One woman who played a significant role in my life when I was a teenager—and, I believe, reinforced my determination to follow my dream—was what we called in that time a woman of ill repute. As children we were told to stay away from her because it was known that men paid for her sexual favors, but, for whatever reason, I used to whisper a greeting when I passed by her house or encountered her on the street.

Shortly after my grandmother died, she stopped by to offer me her sympathies, and we had a conversation. "Do you know why I do what I do?" she asked, and when I indicated that I didn't, she went on. "When I was a young girl, I was fascinated by biology. I wanted to be a scientist, but people kept telling me that I was crazy, women didn't 'do that.' They thought I was getting above myself and told me I should just think about getting a good job as a domestic or a hairdresser. But I didn't want to scrub other people's floors, and I didn't want to stand on my feet all day doing some other woman's hair for a twenty-five-cent tip." So, because she was young and attractive, she did the kind of work that paid the most money for what she determined was the least effort. "It has provided for me," she said. "Do I like what I do? No. But I would rather do this than scrub floors." And she confided that she still thought she would have succeeded in her field of choice if others hadn't killed her dream.

I remembered that conversation, and when it came to following my own heart and my dream of being ordained, it helped me to maintain the confidence I needed to move forward. Even as a child, I was invited to speak at churches, and people were astonished that I never seemed to be nervous about addressing large audiences or speaking extemporaneously without any notes. Their amazement, however, didn't stop them from trying to kill my dream. At the time, it was unheard of for a woman to enter the ministry, and I learned early on that being "young, gifted, and black" did not necessarily mean that you could do or be whatever you wanted. In fact, the only one who supported my dream was my grandmother, and she died when I was twelve.

There were many who tried to dissuade me, including one who quoted the verse from First Timothy where Paul says, "I suffer not a woman to teach, nor to usurp authority over a man, but to be in silence" (1 Timothy 2:12). But that didn't make sense to me. Women were, in fact, far from silent. They taught Sunday school, sang in choirs, and served as missionaries. Why, then, couldn't we also speak from the pulpit?

There were, among the dream-killers, those who told me that no man would want to marry a woman preacher. (They were wrong, too.) When my grandma died these naysayers breathed a sigh of relief, assuming that I would now give up my foolish notion. One family friend in particular seemed to make it her personal mission to discourage me not only from preaching but even from attending college. She was a God-fearing churchgoer of the old school who had no problem letting me know that I was bound to go to hell for trying to do something God intended only for men. Others were a bit more subtle but no less deterring. I was told that because I "spoke well" I'd make a wonderful schoolteacher or that I should consider becoming a social worker.

When I was accepted in the seminary I was a double minority: black and female. My fellow male students seemed uncomfortable having me as a classmate, and when I got straight As, they seemed angry. When I tried to engage them in debate about their attitude toward women in ministry, they quoted unsubstantiated theories about women in general and their place in society. It was extremely frustrating, and I was very grateful when one day a male classmate took me aside and whispered, "Hey, keep on keeping on. Your gift will make room for you."

From that moment on, I have never preached or argued about the place of women in the ministry. I realized that although people tried to kill my dream, they didn't have access to my inner vision, and that I could see with my inner eye that this was my life's calling. Over the years I have gained strength from the words, "Where *there is* no vision, the people perish" (Proverbs 29:18). My only caveat is that you need to be careful about the people with whom you choose to share your dream because they may be dream-killers.

How many people have decided not to try out for a job or a team or a part in a play or a place in an orchestra because others have told them, "You're not good enough. You'll never make it. Why don't you just get real?" I don't know why—perhaps because they have no dreams of their own—but these people seem to build themselves up by taking other people down. What we all need to remember when someone tries to do that to us is that these people can only prevail if we give them the power to do so. People who set themselves up as little gods, claiming to know better than we do what is best for us, do not have God-like powers. If we keep the one true and powerful God in our minds and our hearts, He will lead us on our true path. If, on the other hand, we let others usurp his power, we are invariably led astray. As Jesus said to Matthew, "If ye have faith as a grain of mustard seed . . . nothing shall be impossible unto you" (Matthew 17:20).

LET HIM BE YOUR SUPPORT SYSTEM

Dream-killers, killjoys, come in every size and shape and may turn up anywhere, even within your own family. Some of them actually think they're "doing it for your own good," so that you don't get hurt and disappointed. But whatever their motive, they are destructive, and we need to be strong to resist their admonishments.

It seems that these days there is a support group for every imaginable situation, and sometimes we need a supportive listener to keep us strong when others are dragging us down. But what happens when the one you turn to for support isn't available? What if it's in the middle of the night or the line is busy when you call? Who do you turn to then for support? Well, God is always available. He's on call 24/7, and if you live by His laws He will support you. He will give you the strength to believe in yourself. He won't let anyone kill the joy of your dreams.

COMMANDING THOUGHTS

- Do you kill the joy of others?

- Do not allow killings to make you hateful.

- Do not allow anyone to kill your joy.

- Do not allow anyone to kill your hopes and dreams.

- Use your killer instinct to destroy the negative spirits within you.

- Beware of the company you keep.

- Avoid hostile, hot-tempered people in your life.

CHAPTER SEVEN

"THOU SHALT NOT COMMIT ADULTERY"

EXODUS 20:14

"Even if marriages are made in heaven, man has to be responsible for the maintenance."

—KROEHLER NEWS

What is adultery but the physical manifestation of confusing lust with love, elevating satisfaction of the flesh at the expense of the spirit? When we marry, we vow to take our partner "in sickness and in health, *forsaking all others.*" Although marriage is a union recognized by civil law, and many people have civil ceremonies, the majority of us still say our vows before a clergy person and "in the sight of God." Traditionally (and still in some religious communities) Jewish weddings were actually held in the open air to symbolize the fact that God was looking down upon and blessing the union. His seventh commandment sanctifies marriage.

When someone betrays those vows by committing adultery, that person is committing a sin against the commitment he or she made to his marriage partner. Remember that only a married person can commit adultery; his or her partner in crime is aiding and abetting the sin by engaging in fornication but is not an adulterer. Fornication is sexual intercourse between two people not married to each other, and that, too, is a sin in the eyes of the Lord. Jude, in his Epistle, reminds the people of the fornicator's fate: "Even as Sodom and Gomorrha, and the cities about them in like manner, giving themselves over to fornication, and going after strange flesh, are set forth for an example, suffering the vengeance of eternal fire" (Jude 1:7). So an adulterer is always engaging another person in sin, thereby compounding his or her betrayal.

GOD KNOWS WE ARE SINNERS

Adulterers have always been with us. Even in biblical times King Solomon "had seven hundred wives, princesses, and three hundred concubines: and his wives turned away his heart. For it came to pass, when Solomon was old, *that* his wives turned away his heart after other gods: and his heart was not perfect with the Lord his God, as *was* the heart of David his father" (1 Kings 11:3–4). As a result of his adultery, Solomon turned away from the one true God, "And the Lord was angry with Solomon" (1 Kings 11:9).

When Solomon turned away from God, he was compounding his adultery because he was committing spiritual adultery as well. Many of us are unfaithful in our relationship to God. We make him promises we do not keep. One spiritual adulteress of my acquaintance prayed that her soldier son would return safely from war. She promised God that if He brought her son home to her, she would stop drinking, read her Bible daily, and attend church faithfully. Her prayers were answered; her son came home, and virtually immediately she reneged on her promise.

Instead of attending church that Sunday, she stayed home and prepared a lavish meal for family and friends, complete with alcohol of which she enjoyed her fair share. The following weekend, it was a trip to the casino, and every Sunday thereafter, some activity interfered with her keeping her promise to God. Until, that is, several months later, when she found out she needed an operation that scared her to death. On that occasion she asked if I would pray for her. When I inquired what exactly she wanted from God, she said that, of course, she wanted to be healed and restored to health. And what was she willing to do for God? I asked.

Again, the same litany flowed from her lips: She would pray, read her Bible daily, go to church regularly, and give up all her bad habits. When I reminded her that she'd made and broken these promises before, and that she was being unfaithful to God, she shook her head and said, "I know, I know, I didn't do what I promised. But if He heals me and gives me another chance, I truly will serve Him with all my heart." And this time, she really did remain faithful. She recovered and has been a changed person ever since. She now enjoys what life has to offer in moderation, and, as she put it to me, "God comes first in everything I do."

God asks that we forsake all others and cleave unto Him as He asks us to cleave to our spouse. And when we are unfaithful, God always knows; He knows all. As he commanded Jeremiah to tell the children of the house of Judah, "I have seen thine adulteries, and thy neighings, the lewdness of thy whoredom, *and* thine abominations on the hills in the fields. Woe unto thee, O Jerusalem! wilt thou not be made clean? when *shall it* once be?" (Jeremiah 13:27). And again in Jeremiah 29:23, He says of the false prophets, "Because they have committed villainy in Israel, and have committed adultery with their neighbors' wives, and have spoken lying words in my name, which I have not commanded them; even I know, and *am* a witness." Let these be words to the wise for all who engage in, or are considering, adultery. You may think that you can get away with it, but the Lord will know you as a sinner.

ADULTERY IS A SELFISH ACT

When a criminal is caught and brought before the court, the expression of remorse is, to some degree, considered a mitigating factor. But these days many people consider it their right to have multiple extra-marital partners and often express no remorse at all. In fact, they justify their adultery by stating that it was merely a sexual act with no love involved at all. To me that means it is a purely selfish act with no purpose other than the satisfaction of the flesh. Some go even farther, stating that if sex within marriage becomes "boring," having an affair can add "spice" to the marital relationship. Variety, they say, is the spice of life, and if one marital partner doesn't want to engage in some particular sex act, the other can satisfy his or her urge by going outside the marriage, thereby relieving the reluctant partner from any pressure to do something he or she doesn't want to do. However, no amount of self-justification can alter the fact that adultery is a sin, pure and simple.

One woman I know was married to a wonderful man—that was the very word she used to describe him, *wonderful*—but, she said, his sexual appetite didn't match hers and she enjoyed "getting a little on the side." One day, she met a man who was as "freaky" as she was, and, because her husband happened to be out of town, they had the opportunity to spend the night together. But when she woke up the next morning in a seedy motel with her "freaky" partner next to her, all she could think of was how stupid she had been and how dirty she felt. Not only was this man incapable of having an intelligent conversation, he snored too loudly and hadn't even had the decency to wash himself after the act was over. When, in the cold light of day, she compared him to her husband, she realized what a shameful thing she had done, and she has been trying to rid herself of the guilt ever since.

GOD GAVE US FREE WILL

We humans would like to separate sex from love, satisfaction of the flesh from satisfaction of the spirit, but when we commit ourselves to a monogamous union it is expected that we will uphold that commitment in body, mind, and spirit. We don't get to pick and choose which parts of ourselves we're committing and which parts we're not.

Sin—and particularly the sin of adultery—begins in the mind, with evil thoughts, lustful thoughts and fantasies, and a vivid, lewd imagination. These days, too many of us seem to have our mind in the gutter.

People are obsessed with sex and that obsession has spawned an entire industry of tools and toys designed to satisfy our sexual demons as well as medications designed to enhance sexual activity.

But if lust begins in the mind, so does the ability to make decisions with regard to our actions. God gave us that power so that we don't have to act upon every urge or thought because we can decide not to.

Not only that, but we also have the ability to communicate with each other, to let our marriage partner know what does or doesn't please us. Satisfaction takes place in the mind and the heart as well as the body, and the height of ecstasy results from lovemaking with a committed partner, not from fornication.

LOVELESS LUST LEADS TO LOSS

Many an adulterer will say that if his or her partner doesn't find out about it, no one is being hurt. But that is not true. For one thing, the adulterer knows, and he or she has to get up and look at himself in the mirror in the morning—just like the woman I described previously—and confront the sinner staring back at him.

Because we have the God-given power to choose right or wrong, we also have the God-given burden of knowing when we've made the wrong choice. Knowing that, we automatically lose something—our self-respect—but that's only the beginning. Any sin, including adultery, affects people other than the sinner and thereby compounds the loss.

Adultery is not only a sin, it's a sin committed in secret, and secrets lead to lies, and lies lead to more lies, until we are, in effect, living a lie. The more we lie the harder it is to live in relationship with ourselves, with the marital partner to whom we are lying, and with God. We can't lie to the Lord, so, ultimately, by committing adultery we lose not only our integrity, but also our relationship with our committed partner and our relationship with God.

Adultery can also be costly in purely monetary terms. It can be expensive to cover up the extra costs of "running around," and more than one adulterer has been caught by telltale charges on his or her credit card. Many is the adulterer who thinks he or she is too clever to be caught, but, as we learn in Proverbs 16:18, "Pride *goeth* before destruction, and an haughty spirit before a fall." Only a fool could fail to understand that God's commandments are intended for our edification and to help ensure our success as human beings. And, as the old saying goes, "A fool and his money are soon parted." If you want to throw your money away, that's one thing, but if you're taking that money away from your marriage partner and your family, they, too, are losing something that is rightfully theirs.

And ultimately, ironically, you risk losing your health. How often have I heard adulterers shrug off the importance of their sin by saying, "It was just good healthy sex." But casual sex can lead to some very unhealthy diseases and even death. A study by the Centers for Disease Control and Prevention released in March 2008 revealed that one in four teenage girls in the United States had at least one sexually transmitted disease. And even though HIV may no longer be the death sentence it was when AIDS first came upon the scene, it is still a life-threatening and chronic illness transmitted by the exchange of bodily fluids.

The adulterer who acquires any one of these diseases and then passes it on to a marital partner—or to another adulterous partner—is putting multiple lives at risk.

If you're foolish enough to risk ruining your own life for a few fleeting moments of sexual satisfaction, that's one thing. But if you're thoughtless and insensitive enough to risk ruining the lives of others in order to scratch your sexual itch, you'll need to answer not only to your own conscience but also to the omniscient God who witnessed your sacred vows of marital fidelity.

THE DAMAGE GOES ON AND ON

It would be impossible not to be aware of the damage adultery has done to the lives of so many public figures in recent times. But the adulterous relationships we hear about and see on our television screens are just a tiny percentage of all those that have ruined lives. What we see being played out in public is going on in thousands if not tens of thousands of households every year.

Adulterers humiliate themselves, they humiliate

their partners, and they cause incalculable damage to innocent children, friends, and loved ones in their extended family. Repairing that damage—if at all possible—is always difficult and painful.

Payne found that out the hard way when he and his wife, Cora, came to me for counseling in an attempt to save their marriage. They'd been married for eleven years, during which time Payne had engaged in several adulterous affairs. They still loved each other, but Cora could no longer trust her husband. Every time he left the house and returned, she would want to know "what took you so long? Were you with one of your whores?" And she was also obsessed with knowing every sordid detail of every liaison.

She'd discovered his infidelity when she used his cell phone one day and saw that all his most recent calls had come from one woman whose name she didn't recognize, and she'd looked up the address in the phone book. She said that she'd already become suspicious of Payne's frequent evening outings and was "fed up with his lame excuses." After he left that evening, she drove to the address she'd found, and sure enough, there was his car parked in the light of the apartment building. When he returned home late that night and slipped into bed next to her muttering something about a sports bar and watching a game with the boys, she went berserk. Slapping at him with all her might, she began screaming that she knew where he'd been and kicked him out of the room. After that she refused to speak to him for several days, but if only for the sake of the children, she knew that their situation had to be resolved.

It was Payne who suggested counseling. He wanted to save the marriage, and he knew they couldn't go on that way for much longer.

According to him, the affairs had been meaningless. A couple had been one-night-stands, one was an on-again, off-again office romance that ended after several months, and some he couldn't remember at all. He swore that he didn't love anyone but Cora but said, "Women have always been my weakness. I just like sex." He'd apologized to her over and over, but she was unimpressed, declaring, "You're only sorry because you got caught."

Payne and Cora were married when they were both in their late twenties, and Payne said he fell in love with her because she was "good and good looking" and he knew she didn't mess around. He didn't want to marry a woman who'd been intimate with guys he knew or who they might run into as a couple. He acknowledged that Cora was a wonderful wife, an excellent homemaker, and a great mother to their young son and daughter. He had never wanted to hurt her and declared that he'd never had any intention of leaving her—to which Cora responded bitterly, "You want to have your cake and eat it, too." To her he didn't seem sufficiently contrite, and she didn't think he fully understood the extent of her pain and her shame. She heard his words but didn't believe they came from his heart. And, to make matters worse from her point of view, "He has the nerve to expect me to have sex with him!"

I suggested that, since they both wanted to save the relationship, they should go away for a weekend together and try to rekindle the bond. At the same time I warned Payne that he should neither expect nor press Cora to engage in sex. It was important that they simply relearn what it was like to enjoy being together.

They needed to have some fun and try not to talk about their problem.

When I saw them next, Payne didn't seem too happy with the results of their little experiment. He said that Cora had cried and kept making sarcastic remarks. When I asked him for an example, he told me that whenever they saw a happy or affectionate couple she would remark, "I wonder if that's his wife or his woman." Much as he'd tried, he said, nothing he'd done seemed to please her.

It was now time for Cora to decide what she was willing to do and what concessions she was willing to make for the sake of reconciliation. "Not a damn thing," she stated, firmly and flatly. "I'm the one he hurt and deceived. I can't compete with those women, and I'm not even going to try." She was particularly furious to think that Payne's selfish pleasures might have put her at risk for contracting a sexually transmitted disease.

In subsequent sessions, we talked about forgiveness, about God's forgiving love and compassion, and about his wish that we forgive one another as He forgives us.

I encouraged Cora to pray for some peace and tranquillity because if she couldn't find that, her overwhelming anger would eventually destroy her. For Payne, the task was to accept the error of his ways, develop a closer spiritual relationship with God, and learn to resist temptation. Even for the most deeply religious, temptation is likely to rear its ugly head at the most unexpected moments, and there is always a price to pay for giving in—particularly to temptations of the flesh.

After seven months of intensive counseling, Cora decided that she wanted a divorce. At that point, the pain she'd been wanting Payne to feel all along finally surfaced. He was stunned. He couldn't believe that after all he'd tried to do to make amends, this was the result. But Cora didn't feel he'd given up his philandering because he knew in his heart it was right; she believed that he thought he was "making a supreme sacrifice" just to save the marriage. She wasn't angry anymore but she didn't think she'd ever be able to regain her trust in or respect for him. She would always love "the Payne I fell in love with," but the adulterous Payne was a total stranger to her.

Payne is still in counseling and says that he now

has no desire for anyone but his former wife. But he also realizes that Cora has moved on and is glad she's found peace, because, he says, "I haven't." As he told me at the end of one session, "It wasn't worth it, Doc. I blew it for nothing."

COMMITMENT IS FOR THE LONG TERM

Sadly, we've become a society that expects instant gratification and subscribes to the notion of built-in obsolescence. When we see something we want, we buy it (even if we can't afford it) and when the next, better model comes along, we discard the first one and buy the newer one.

We use the word *love* very loosely these days. We "love" a car or a piece of jewelry or a fancy new cell phone, and then, a little while later, we love a different car, or a newer piece of jewelry, or an even fancier phone.

Unfortunately, a lot of people seem to take the same approach to relationships. When we commit to another person in marriage, however, it's not supposed to work that way.

As Jesus explained to the Pharisees with relation to God's creation in Matthew 19:4–6:

Have ye not read, that he which made them *at the*
beginning made them male and female, And said,
   For this cause shall a man leave father and
   mother, and shall cleave to his wife:
   and they twain shall be one flesh?
Wherefore they are no more twain, but one flesh.
What therefore God hath joined together, let not
man put asunder.

And Shakespeare put it beautifully in Sonnet 116:

Let me not to the marriage of true minds
Admit impediments. Love is not love
Which alters when it alteration finds,
Or bends with the remover to remove.
O, no, it is an ever-fixèd mark
That looks on tempests and is never shaken;
It is the star to every wand'ring bark,
Whose worth's unknown, although his height be
   taken.

Love's not Time's fool, though rosy lips and cheeks
Within his bending sickle's compass come;
Love alters not with his brief hours and weeks,
But bears it out even to the edge of doom.
If this be error and upon me proved,
I never writ, nor no man ever loved.

Love, in other words, rests in the mind. We do not stop loving because our loved one ages or sickens. The flesh is subject to the whims of time but the mind and heart are not. Paradoxically, that's why diseases like Alzheimer's are so devastating: The one we love is physically present but the person we love has gone from us.

If we don't understand that kind of commitment, we don't understand the nature of true love.

COMMANDING THOUGHTS

- If you are in a marital or monogamous relationship with someone, are you faithful to that person?

- What can you do to establish loyalty and fidelity in your relationship?

- Are you guilty of loving one person and lusting after another?

- How can you deal with the temptation to stray from your commitment?

- Are you true to God?

- Does He deserve anything less than your total love and obedience to His law?

CHAPTER EIGHT

"THOU SHALT NOT STEAL"

EXODUS 20:15

> *"The power of choosing good and evil is within the reach of all."*
>
> —ORIGEN, *De Principiis*, Alexander Roberts
> and James Donaldson, translators

On one level, this commandment seems pretty simple and straightforward: If it doesn't belong to you, you can't take it. But the more we think about it, the more complex and thought-provoking the commandment becomes. When we think about stealing, the first thing that comes to mind is taking some tangible "thing" that belongs to someone else—that is, theft of property. And, of course, no one has the right to take another person's property. But in these times, even property theft has risen to a whole new level. It's not just burglary or purse-snatching anymore. Now it's car-jacking, stealing social security checks out of mailboxes, stealing money from church collection boxes, and, on the highest level, corporate theft that literally steals the life savings of employees and stock holders.

We humans are very clever; it's amazing how many ways we've thought of and what lengths we'll go to in order to take what isn't ours. The most audacious and outrageous thefts are the stuff that entertainment is made of—think of smash box office hit movies like *Topkapi* and *Ocean's Eleven*. The smarter and slyer the thieves are, the bigger the prize they're going after, the more we admire and root for them to succeed. The entertainment media have, in fact, gone a long way toward representing big-time stealing as glamorous. In real life, however, it's a very different story.

For example, just as clever and audacious, the ways people have come up with to steal from us via the Internet, would have been unthinkable just a few years ago. But in real life there are real victims, and the thieves don't look like movie stars.

WHERE DO YOU DRAW THE LINE?

The term *petty larceny* is a legal term referring to the theft of items below a certain value. There are all kinds of ways to indulge in all kinds of petty theft. Taking money out of a parent's wallet or a child's piggy bank is a particularly ignominious form of petty theft. When we conduct personal business on the computer at work, we're stealing time our employer has paid for. When we take home supplies like pens and paper clips, we're stealing. If we take credit for another person's work, that's also theft.

Since so much information is now available to all through electronic media, intellectual property law has become a cutting edge area of practice for attorneys. But long before the Internet, there have been those who prospered by stealing other people's ideas. This can be either a passive act, like standing silent without giving credit where credit is due, or it can be the active and deliberate appropriation of another person's work product. I often wonder why people who are clever enough to think up so many innovative ways to steal other people's ideas don't think of spending that time to come up with ideas of their own.

Some people seem to think it's okay to steal from a big institution because "they'll never miss it." So, if they're given too much change in a store or if the cash machine in a bank dispenses twice as much money as it should have, they count themselves lucky and consider it a "victimless crime." They don't even think of it as stealing—but it is.

The problem is that once you get away with something, it becomes easier to do it again. Or, to put it another way, once you've disobeyed one of God's commandments, why not move on to disobeying another? The more we consider the commandments, the better we are able to understand how one relates to every other one. We see that very clearly when Hosea conveys to the children of Israel the punishment to be inflicted on them by God because of their transgressions against Him: "Hear the word of the Lord, ye children of Israel: for the Lord hath a controversy with the inhabitants of the land, because *there is* no truth, nor mercy, nor knowledge of God in the land. By swearing, and lying, and killing, and stealing, and committing adultery, they break out, and blood toucheth blood. Therefore shall the land mourn, and every one that dwelleth therein shall languish" (Hosea 4:1–3). Once the people turned away from the "knowledge of God," they didn't stop at breaking one commandment, but proceeded to break them all. When Hosea wrote those words in 781 BC, the people had abandoned the laws of their Creator, and, sadly, we seem to be in a similar state of lawlessness today.

Old folks used to say, very wisely, "If you lie you will steal, and if you steal you will lie, and if you lie you will kill." In other words, where does it stop?

In fact, innumerable deaths have occurred because a thief was caught in the act and panicked. The perpetrator then cries that he or she didn't mean that to happen. But the fact is that the victim is dead, and the thief should have thought about the potential consequences before deciding to steal.

REV. DR. ARLENE CHURN

THERE'S MORE TO "THINGS"
THAN THEIR FACE VALUE

When you steal another person's possessions, you're also depriving him of all the time and effort, all the hard work that went into creating, building, or acquiring those things. That's like taking away a piece of a person's life. We like to think that things are just things, and we often hear victims say, "I still have my health. I can always buy another (whatever it is). But what if you can't? What about people who've worked long and hard for what they've got and who simply don't have the wherewithal to replace it? Or what if the thing that's stolen is irreplaceable?

A thief will steal your purse or your wallet, take the money, and throw the "thing" in the nearest trash can. But what if there are precious photos of lost loved ones in that purse or wallet? What if the necklace or bracelet that's stolen was given to you or inherited from a loved one who's passed on?

While we certainly shouldn't overvalue our possessions or allow them to define us, there are things whose value isn't monetary but that may, nevertheless, be "more precious far than gold"—even though they may be meaningless and useless to the one who steals them.

TRUST IS A PRECIOUS COMMODITY

These days, many people live with burglar alarms, dead bolts, multiple locks, and whatever other antitheft devices they can think of to protect their belongings. There are surveillance cameras in public places and identity cards just to get into the office buildings we frequent every day. What we've all lost, however, is the trust we used to have when times were simpler and we didn't have to worry so much. Doors were left unlocked, bicycles were left in driveways, neighbors looked out for one another.

Now, in restaurants, shops, or even at large gatherings in someone's home, we keep a watchful eye on our purse or our wallet. We no longer trust that if we leave our money unattended, even for a moment, it will be safe.

To me, among the vilest thefts are the ones committed against those who are most trusting and most vulnerable—our senior citizens. Scam artists befriend these people—who are most often women—win their trust, and then steal their life savings. In most cases it's as easy as stealing candy from a baby. And almost always the victim laments that "he seemed like such a nice young man," or, "I don't know how I could have been so trusting."

Trust in our fellow humans is a terrible thing to lose, and losing trust in those who are closest to us, our family members, is the most devastating loss of all.

Matt was the thirty-one-year-old spoiled and eldest son of loving parents who gave him everything he wanted. Sadly, when he went away to college he fell in with a bad group of friends who introduced him to drugs, and within a short time, Matt was addicted. His parents could see that something about him had changed, but the idea that he might have a drug problem never entered their minds, even when he began to ask for larger and larger sums of money.

Matt was good at covering up his problem, and he kept telling his parents that he needed money for various business investments that always, for one reason or another, went bad. First it was supposed to be a video rental franchise, then a company selling refurbished computers. Each time he assured them that the venture "couldn't fail," and each time he came up with a series of lame excuses when, of course, it did.

In fact, Matt had never "invested" the money at all in anything other than drugs. When his parents finally told him that they simply couldn't afford another failed investment, he went into a deep depression. He lost weight and became extremely nervous and short-tempered. His parents begged him to see a doctor, but, of course, he couldn't do that without being found out.

Eventually his parents began to notice that various items of value were missing from their home, and when they tentatively questioned Matt, he actually tried to convince them that they were becoming forgetful and were perhaps no longer capable of handling their own affairs. By now they realized that he had a serious problem, but they still didn't know what it could be.

One day not too long after that, Matt's parents received a phone call from the police. Matt had been found semiconscious in his car with drug paraphernalia lying next to him. He had overdosed and was taken to the hospital. When he recovered and appeared in court, he was put on probation and ordered to enter a drug program. Matt spent the next month at a private rehabilitation facility paid for by his parents. When he got out and returned home, he managed to stay clean for two months before relapsing. Now it was his parents' turn to cry, beg, and plead with him to get his life in order. He promised that he "had it under control" and that he'd be "all right." But he wasn't.

As the firstborn son, Matt was a "junior," which made it easy for him to steal blank checks from his father and forge his name, as well as to appropriate one of his credit cards. He then stole the mail so that his parents would not receive their bank and credit card statements. When his father eventually realized something was wrong and looked into the matter, the jig was up for Matt. His parents were furious that he would steal from them "after all we've done for you!" They told him that unless he got help immediately, they'd have nothing more to do with him—ever—and that this time he'd have to do it on his own.

The state-funded facility he signed himself into this time was far less comfortable than the private rehab his parents had paid for. But he stuck it out and when he was released he returned home only to find that his parents wouldn't let him into their house. "We are still hurt, and we just don't trust you," they said.

It was then that Matt determined to seek counseling. He wanted to prove to his parents that he had really changed this time. He wanted to regain their respect and love and, above all, their trust, but first he had to learn to trust himself. In our sessions we discussed Matt's stealing, and he had a hard time thinking of himself as a thief. Instead, he blamed his actions on his drug problem. It took a while for him to be able to concede that he was responsible for the choices he had made.

At that time, he was working in an outlet store at a local mall. He wasn't earning very much money, but for the first time in his life he was disciplined, getting himself to work every day, and learning to live on a limited budget. I suggested that he send his parents money each time he got paid. How much he could send didn't really matter; the point was to show his parents that he had good intentions.

I told him that very often we continue to punish ourselves long after God has forgiven us, and I suggested that he needed to forgive himself. In addition, I encouraged him to seek strength from the Lord. As I explained to Matt, since Christ came to earth and died for our sins, we now live by His grace, which means that God will forgive us if we but petition Him through prayer. This knowledge seemed to bring him some peace, but he was still distraught over his parents' rejection.

At his request, they accompanied him to his last counseling session. Matt knew that just as he had asked God's forgiveness, he now needed to ask for theirs. They were a handsome couple in their mid-fifties, who told me that they had worked hard and invested their money wisely, and that Matt had almost ruined them financially. They were still at a loss to understand why he'd done what he did, stating sadly that "we didn't raise him to steal," and that "he could have come to us when he realized he had a problem." Matt could only repeat that he'd thought he had his addiction under control, and when I saw how the conversation was going, I intervened to stop them from rehashing what was past and to encourage them to focus on how they were going to move forward.

Matt only wanted a chance to prove that he was trustworthy and to regain his parents' love. They, of course, had never stopped loving him and said that they wanted very badly to trust him. For the first time in more than a year they were able to hug one another, and Matt's father finally said, "We can recover from the loss of money, but we can never get another son."

I'm happy to report that Matt is still drug free, doing well, and has met a wonderful, understanding woman. They both have a loving relationship with his parents and never speak of his past.

IDENTITY, THE MOST PRECIOUS OF OUR POSSESSIONS

You may be familiar with these lines from Shakespeare's *Othello*:

> *He who steals my purse steals trash; 'tis*
> *something, nothing;*

'Twas mine, 'tis his, and has been slave to
  thousands,
But he that filches from me my good name
Robs me of that which not enriches him,
And makes me poor indeed.

Ironically, those words are spoken by Iago, one of the biggest liars in all of literature. But Iago got it only partly right, because stealing another person's good name not only makes him poor but also, in most cases, enriches the thief—at least until he or she is caught.

These days stealing another person's good name isn't just a matter of stealing a purse with identification in it; it's about co-opting the victim's identity by gaining access to his or her most precious personal information. We're constantly being told not to give out our personal information over the phone or on the Internet, and most of us have become vigilant about guarding our social security number, our bank account numbers—all those numbers and "secret" passwords we need just to conduct business on a daily basis. But the more vigilant we are, it seems, the smarter the thieves become. And once someone has stolen our good name in order to use it instead of their bad one to establish credit, it's extremely difficult to prove that we are who we are and get back our rightful name. Just a few years ago, that would have seemed unthinkable, but these days the numbers are frightening. A 2003 survey sponsored by the Federal Trade Commission estimated that almost 10 million Americans had been victims of ID theft in the past year and almost 27 million in the past five years. These crimes meant a total loss to businesses, who were also victims of the theft, of almost $50 billion, and a cost to the victims themselves of about $5 billion, not to mention the 300 million hours spent trying to resolve the problems. And the numbers are growing exponentially.

STEALING FROM GOD, THE MOST HEINOUS THEFT OF ALL

"Will a man rob God? Yet ye have robbed me. But ye say, Wherein have we robbed thee? In tithes and offerings" (Malachi 3:8).

Many people find tithing onerous; they don't believe they should have to give back any of their hard-earned money, even to the Lord. What they're missing out on is the promise that comes with the offering: "Bring ye all the tithes into the storehouse, that there may be meat in mine house, and prove me now herewith, saith the Lord of hosts, if I will not open you the windows of heaven, and pour you out a blessing, that *there shall* not *be room* enough *to receive it*" (Malachi 3:10). Whatever we offer to Him comes back to us many times.

Make no mistake, God doesn't need our money. In fact, He doesn't need anything from us at all. But He wants us to prosper, and the surest way we have to do that is to be obedient to His commands. He wants us to be givers rather than takers. I remember standing on the banks of the Dead Sea several years ago and remarking to our tour guide how dark, oily, and full of debris the water appeared. He told me that this was because the sea couldn't throw off anything it received. It was dead and, therefore, incapable of creating or sustaining life of any kind. I couldn't help thinking, then, of all those people who take, take, take and give nothing in return, and whose lives, therefore, do not grow or flourish.

With this commandment, God is telling us: Taking from others what is not rightfully yours will never enrich you in any way. Even if you increase your material wealth, you will be morally and spiritually bankrupt. Even if you think you've gotten away with your crime, He will know what you have done.

In Revelations 22:12, 14 we are told that Christ will return to earth to judge mankind: "And, behold, I come quickly; and my reward *is* with me, to give every man according as his work shall be. . . . Blessed *are* they that do his commandments, that they may have right to the tree of life, and may enter in through the gates into the city." And in 2 Peter 3:10 we learn how he will come. Ironically, we are told that "the day of the Lord will come as a thief in the night," which means that we ought to live righteously at all times and "be diligent that ye may be found of him in peace, without spot, and blameless" (2 Peter 3:14) because we never know when that judgment will be upon us.

COMMANDING THOUGHTS

- Commit to honesty in all areas of your life.

- Do not engage in petty thefts and believe that you are justified.

- Have you ever stolen another person's thoughts or ideas?

- Do you take without giving back?

- Have you stolen from God?

- Have you allowed someone to "steal your heart" away from the Lord?

- Be careful to whom you give your heart.

CHAPTER NINE

"THOU SHALT NOT BEAR FALSE WITNESS AGAINST THY NEIGHBOUR"

EXODUS 20:16

"I will speak ill of no man, and speak all the good I know of everybody."

—BENJAMIN FRANKLIN

Basically, God is telling us here that we need to tell the truth. We cannot lie, but, more specifically, we can't tell a lie that's going to get someone else into trouble. Little children do that all the time. When Mommy says, "Who drew on the wall with crayon?" Suzy points to Johnny and says, "He did it," even though Johnny is totally innocent and Suzy knows perfectly well she's the culprit. By the time we're adults, however, bearing false witness can do a lot more harm than mommy's spanking the wrong kid.

Reputations are ruined, jobs can be lost, people are driven apart, and, at worst, the wrong person goes to prison for a crime he or she didn't commit. God knew what terrible injustice could follow upon bearing false witness and, therefore, forbade us to tell untruths about others.

Jesus himself was betrayed by false witnesses, first before Caiaphas the high priest as we learn in Matthew 26:60–61: "At the last came two false witnesses, And said, This *fellow* said, I am able to destroy the temple of God, and to build it in three days." And again by Peter, who denies him three times as Jesus had prophesied he would: "Now Peter sat without in the palace: and a damsel came unto him, saying, Thou also wast with Jesus of Galilee. But he denied before *them* all, saying, I know not what thou sayest. And when he was gone out into the porch, another *maid* saw him, and said unto them that were there, This *fellow* was also with Jesus of Nazareth. And again he denied with an oath, I do not know the man. And after a while came unto *him* they that stood by, and said to Peter, Surely thou also art *one* of them; for thy speech betrayeth thee. Then began he to curse and to swear, saying, I know not the man. And immediately the cock crew. And Peter remembered the word of Jesus, which said unto him, Before the cock crow, thou shalt deny me thrice. And he went out, and wept bitterly" (Matthew 26:69–75).

Jesus is subsequently brought before Pilate, who must decide whether to release him or another prisoner, Barabbas, as was customary on Passover. The crowd that has gathered, including the chief priests and elders, call for the release of Barabbas and the death of Jesus. And even when Pilate asks, "Why, what evil hath he done?" he knows that "he could prevail nothing, but *that* rather a tumult was made" (Matthew 27:23–24). In other words, even the governor's attempt at reason was powerless in the face of the prevailing mob mentality.

This scene is a bitter precursor of other historic instances, including the infamous Salem witch trials, in which a mob bearing false witness caused the loss of innocent lives.

The commandments are all about preserving social order, living in harmony not only with the Lord but with one another. In fact, it is by living in harmony with God's laws that we are able to live harmoniously together. When we lose the light of truth by bearing false witness, we lose our way. As Jesus said to the Jews in John 8:32, "The truth shall make you free."

TAKING THE OATH

The commandments are the foundation on which law is built, and as King David asks in Psalm 11, "If the foundations be destroyed, what can the righteous do?"

When we bear witness in a court of law we take an oath swearing to tell the truth, the whole truth, and nothing but the truth. In fact, the law is very clear about what we can attest to as a witness. It must be something of which we have first-hand knowledge. If we attempt to pass on something of which we don't have first-hand knowledge, that information is considered "hear-say" and is disallowed.

When we agree to live according to God's commandments, we are, in effect, taking an oath or making a promise to live a truthful life. So the minute we fail to live up to that promise by telling a lie, we are breaking our oath to Him.

Whether in a court of law or in the larger court of life, however, there are many among us who happily swear to tell the truth and then think nothing of lying through their teeth. Bearing false witness in court is particularly heinous because doing so can (and often does) result in a righteous person's losing his or her freedom. But telling an untruth about another person can have devastating consequences in all circumstances.

ONE LIE LEADS TO ANOTHER

There's an old saying in African American culture that "the dog that brings a bone will carry a bone," meaning that someone who comes to you with gossip will also gossip about you. The fact is that gossips thrive on spreading stories. Even though they're likely to preface their tasty tidbit with the disingenuous claim that they "hate to be the bearer of bad news," the fact is that if they really hated it, they wouldn't be doing it in the first place.

Gossip is a particularly dangerous way of bearing false witness that often begins with someone starting a rumor about another person. There could be any number of reasons, from jealousy to self-protection, to just plain malice. But whatever the reason, all it takes is one falsehood whispered in the ear of another for the lie to take on a life of its own. Just like the game of Telephone we used to play as children, the words get distorted and the story is embellished until what started as a rumor is being accepted as fact. Unlike that children's game, however, gossip can have serious consequences. The poor soul who is the victim of the falsehood often has no way of tracing it back to its roots, to the person who started the rumor, and sometimes no way of knowing why people are suddenly turning against him or her.

I saw this first-hand a few years ago when a lovely young woman named Alexis came to me for counseling out of sheer desperation. She had married her college sweetheart, Tom, who was a career military officer, and during his last overseas tour she had been home alone caring for their three young children. She kept herself busy with her job as a medical transcriber and got involved with the children's school and other activities. She didn't have much to do with Tom's family, and, as she put it, that was fine with her because she found them too nosy and too intrusive—particularly when it came to her marriage and her personal business. In addition, until Alexis put her foot down, Tom had been constantly "lending" money to his mother and his two brothers. Then, when he'd finally agreed to limit his "financial aid," his mother was infuriated and warned Alexis that she'd be sorry for influencing Tom against her.

When Tom finally came home after eighteen months, Alexis noticed a change in his attitude but chalked it up to his need for a period of readjustment and vowed to be patient. Over the next two months, however, he grew even more distant and short-tempered, and when she finally asked what was bothering him, he spit out, "I know all about your little secret affair while I was gone." Alexis was flabbergasted. Not only had she not had an affair, but she had never even thought in passing about the possibility of being unfaithful. When she insisted he tell her how he "knew all about it," he said that his mother had told him. "She saw you with another man on several occasions, including once in your car and once going into a motel." Then he went on to say that since his return several of his relatives and buddies had told him the same story.

Deeply hurt that her husband would believe such a vicious lie, she went to confront her mother-in-law, who repeated that she'd seen Alexis pull into a motel parking lot and wait in the car while the man went into the office to "get the room." Suddenly the light dawned. The "man" was Alexis's step-brother, who had come to town with his girlfriend to attend a wedding. In fact, he and his girlfriend were both in the wedding party and Alexis had driven him to the motel from the airport to book a social room for the bachelor party. When she told her mother-in-law all this, the older woman simply replied, "Well, it sure didn't look that way to me. I only know what I saw with my own two eyes." And, apparently without feeling the need to verify what she had "seen" with her daughter-in-law, she had committed her eye-witness account to paper and sent it in a letter to her son.

When Alexis returned home, furious but certain that she'd simply tell Tom what had really happened and it would all be over, he just looked at her and said, "My mother saw you at a motel, in the car, with a man," and then proceeded to accuse her of further liaisons of which his mother had hinted. He claimed that his "whole family" knew of her affairs, and when she wondered aloud how they could believe such lies, he stated, "My mother told them, just like she told me. People ought to know how you play around when I'm away."

As a last resort, Alexis prevailed upon Tom to accompany her to his mother's house while she spoke to his family about what they allegedly "knew." At the family meeting, she asked his mother to repeat exactly what she thought she had witnessed, and as she spoke, her story very quickly began to unravel. For example, at the time she said she had seen Alexis in the car, the wedding was actually in progress and Alexis had photographs to prove it. Then Tom's mother confessed that she couldn't actually remember who was in the driver's seat. Finally, even her sons realized she was wrong and told her so.

At that point Alexis walked out and went home to pack. She was preparing to leave for good when Tom rushed in, apologizing profusely. Although she didn't leave that day, she was much too hurt and upset to forgive him.

When she came to me for the first time, Alexis was still hurt and confused. She loved her husband but feared that the bond of trust between them had been damaged beyond repair. I suggested that she bring Tom to our next session, and when they arrived he asked quietly and politely what I knew about their situation. Before I had a chance to respond, however, Alexis screamed, "She knows it all. I told her everything!" He seemed embarrassed and began to apologize for his mother, adding that it was difficult for him not to believe her, especially when she said she'd personally witnessed the tryst.

I reminded Tom of the seven things that are an abomination to the Lord: "These six *things* doth the Lord hate: yea seven *are* an abomination unto him: A proud look, a lying tongue, and hands that shed innocent blood, An heart that deviseth wicked imaginations, feet that be swift in running to mischief, A false witness *that* speaketh lies, and he that soweth discord among brethren" (Proverbs 6:16–19). Together we then ticked off the five abominations of which his mother was guilty: a lying tongue, a heart that deviseth wicked imaginations, feet that be swift in running to mischief,

THE POWER OF THE 10

being a false witness, and sowing discord among her brethren. I added that I assumed she hadn't actually shed any blood, and, since I hadn't been there to see it, I couldn't attest to whether or not her look had been proud when she told her untruths.

Tom understood that he had been complicit in his mother's troublemaking, and I suggested that in the future he listen more carefully to the small voice within us all that always speaks the truth.

It was particularly wounding to him as well as to Alexis that all his mother's troublemaking had been undertaken in retribution for his refusing to give her money to buy a fur coat or take a cruise, both of which were luxuries he could ill afford to indulge.

In the end, Tom requested a transfer to another base so that they wouldn't be living so near his family and would also put some distance between themselves and those who still believed his mother's lies. Before leaving, they formally renewed their marital vows and said that the words now had more meaning for them than they did the first time they spoke them. Renewal of their trust in and devotion to each other was also a testimony to their renewal of trust in and devotion to God.

SPEAKING IN SPIRIT

In many communities "snitchin" is not only a much debated and controversial subject but is also often misunderstood and thus misconstrued. Many see "snitchin" as akin to gossip or being a "tattletale," which is considered to be of a malicious nature. We don't want to be guilty of revealing intimate information, whether we heard it firsthand or from a friend. Law enforcement officials however, view "snitchin"— reporting a crime and, perhaps, being a witness against those crimes in a court of law—as a valuable tool in assisting them in apprehending criminals.

The campaign to "stop snitchin" was originated in the Harlem community in New York City, by a man named Shaheed. The popularity of his "stop snitchin" T-shirts gained national recognition in 2004. The message was embraced by several rappers and hip-hop artists and it was used in neighborhoods across the country to intimidate would-be witnesses not to come forth with any damaging information.

I had a client come to me with a unique concern about "snitchin." Sianna was a beautiful thirty-two-year-old single woman who loved her family dearly. A close family member had confided in her that he was planning to commit suicide and Sianna was convinced of his intent to do so. Sianna was overwhelmed with whether she should share this information with other family members. She was concerned about betraying the confidence of her suicidal relative and she did not want to be looked upon as a "snitch."

I advised Sianna that snitching for the sake of mere gossip is both vile and dangerous. However, snitching for the intent to aid or help an individual can be viewed as beneficial. I told her that the fact that her relative had confided in her was probably a call for help. Sianna was further advised to encourage her suicidal relative to enlist the help of a mental health professional rather than simply share his plight with others. Sianna would have been seen as a "hearsay" witness to the possibility of a suicide, and her relative might have denied Sianna's account of the shared conversation, which in turn, would have damaged her credibility. Sianna agreed with the advice given to her, and she pledged that she would support her beloved cousin in resuming his zest for life, in spite of his depression and disappointment.

BE A WITNESS FOR GOD

When we follow God's commandments, we bear witness and testify to His power. In Isaiah 43:10 we read the following: "Ye *are* my witnesses, saith the Lord, and my servant whom I have chosen: that ye may know and believe me, and understand that I *am* he: before me there was no God formed, neither shall there be after me."

Part of the traditional black Baptist worship service used to be the testimony devotion period during which worshippers would rise and testify publicly to God's goodness throughout their trials and tribulations. Proudly, they bore witness to the fact that "the Lord will make a way somehow," or that "you don't know like I know what the Lord has done for me," or, most joyfully, "my soul is a witness for my Lord."

Centuries before live media coverage of events around the world, there were those who bore witness to and recorded the miracles Jesus performed on earth.

And still there are miracles occurring every day, such as the long-awaited birth of a baby to a loving young couple I knew. Their baby was born very prematurely, weighing less than two pounds, and the odds of her surviving were poor. She remained in the neonatal intensive care unit of the hospital for almost five months while her parents prayed along with me and many others. Slowly, miraculously, the baby began to thrive and gain weight. Today she's healthy, has caught up developmentally with others in her age group, and shows no lasting effects of her early ordeal. Since her miraculous survival, the baby's parents have returned to the hospital Neonatal ICU many times to share their story and show their photographs to other worried parents, thereby bearing witness to their answered prayers.

Instead of rushing to repeat a bit of gossip or indulge in spreading a rumor, God asks that we bear witness to His truth. In certain instances, witnesses who put themselves in danger by telling the truth in court are given safe haven by entering the witness protection program. But the Lord has a witness protection program of His own, for, as we are told in Psalm

91:9–11, "Because thou hast made the Lord, *which is* my refuge, *even* the most High, thy habitation; There shall no evil befall thee, neither shall any plague come nigh thy dwelling. For he shall give his angels charge over thee, to keep thee in all thy ways."

COMMANDING THOUGHTS

- Are you a good neighbor?

- Do you think before you speak?

- Is what you know worth repeating?

- It is not always appropriate to tell everything you see, think, or know.

- Is repeating what you have witnessed beneficial to anyone?

- Will it harm anyone unnecessarily or undeservedly?

- Speak only the truth at all times.

- Do not allow a false witness to persuade you into believing a lie.

CHAPTER TEN

"THOU SHALT NOT COVET"

EXODUS 20:17

"Abundance consists not so much in material posses-sions, but in an uncovetous spirit."

—JOHN SELDEN, English jurist

God went into a lot of detail on this one, telling us exactly what we should not covet—our neighbor's wife, nor his house, nor his man- or maid-servant, nor his ox, nor *anything* that is our neighbor's. The word *covet* isn't used much these days. We tend to talk more about envy, jealousy, or an obsessive desire to have what others have and we don't, but the mean-ing is the same.

It's interesting that this commandment follows di-rectly after the one forbidding us to steal. When we covet something that isn't ours—when we're envious, jealous, dissatisfied—that can lead directly to stealing whatever it is we covet just because we want it.

In the book of Joshua we have a good example of what God deems just punishment for those who steal what they covet. The Lord was angry with the children of Israel because one among them had taken spoils from the fallen city of Jericho. So He said to Joshua, "*There is* an accursed thing in the midst of thee, O Israel: thou canst not stand before thine enemies, until ye take away the accursed thing from among you" (Joshua 7:13). The next morning, Joshua called each of the tribes before him, one by one, and when Achan came before him, he said, "My son, give, I pray thee, glory to the Lord God of Israel, and make confession unto him; and tell me now what thou hast done; hide *it* not from me. And Achan answered Joshua, and said, Indeed I have sinned against the Lord God of Israel, and thus and thus have I done: When I saw among the spoils a goodly Babylonish garment, and two hundred shekels of silver, and a wedge of gold of fifty shekels weight, then I coveted them, and took them; and, behold, they *are* hid in the earth in the midst of my tent, and the silver under it. So

Joshua sent messengers, and they ran unto the tent; and, behold, *it* was hid in his tent, and the silver under it" (Joshua 7:19–22).

Today, our young people are on a rampage, stealing high-priced sneakers, fancy jackets, and designer jeans because they feel entitled to them even though they can't afford to buy them. And their greed all too often leads to unnecessary violence, even death. This is one area where parents must lead by example, teaching them to be satisfied with what they have instead of trying to keep up with the Joneses even if it means going heavily into debt.

This state of affairs is nothing new, however, because, as we read in the Epistle of James, written in the first century AD: "From whence *come* wars and fightings among you? *come they* not hence, *even* of your lusts that war in your members? Ye lust, and have not: ye kill, and desire to have, and cannot obtain: ye fight and war, yet ye have not, because ye ask not. Ye ask, and receive not, because ye ask amiss, that ye may consume *it* upon your lusts. . . . Do ye think that the scripture saith in vain, The spirit that dwelleth in us lusteth to envy?" (James 4:1–3, 5).

We must remember that all God's commandments are designed as guidelines to help us lead moral lives. This one deals directly with the accumulation of material goods and the unequal distribution of wealth. God is letting us know that there will always be people who have more than others (the "haves" and the "have nots" as we call them today) and that the value of our life is not dependent upon or judged solely by the value of our possessions. This is made clear in a biblical passage where Jesus is addressing what is described as "an innumerable multitude of people." When one among them asks him to intervene with his brother about sharing his inheritance, Jesus replies, "Take heed, and beware of covetousness: for a man's life consisteth not in the abundance of the things which he possesseth." And he then goes on to relate the parable of the rich fool: "The ground of a certain rich man brought forth plentifully: And he thought within himself, saying, What shall I do, because I have no room where to bestow my fruits? And he said, This will I do: I will pull down my barns, and build greater; and there will I bestow all my fruits and my goods. And I will say to my soul, Soul, thou hast much goods laid up for many years; take thine ease, eat, drink, *and* be merry. But God said unto him, *Thou* fool, this night thy soul shall be required of thee: then whose shall those things be, which thou hast provided? So *is* he that layeth up treasure for himself, and is not rich toward God" (Luke 12:15–21). In other words, in the end, what does it matter how many riches you have acquired if you have not lived a good life in obedience to God.

DESIRE SHOULD MOTIVATE, NOT FRUSTRATE

The admonishment against coveting, does not, how-ever, mean that those with less must look upon their lack as a life sentence. There's nothing wrong with wanting more than you have at the moment. Seeing that others have more than you can be just the inspira-tion you need to work harder, smarter, and longer to better yourself and your position in life. King Solomon, who was rich not only in worldly goods but also in godly wisdom, saw the greed and lust for worldly goods among the people, and provided spiritual insight into the error of their ways: "The desire of the slothful killeth him; for his hands refuse to labour. He coveteth greedily all the day long: but the righteous giveth and spareth not" (Proverbs 21:25–26).

In fact, wanting more for our children—for the next generation—than we have has always been the basis on which the American dream has been built. This is the land of plenty, and, luckily, there's more than one of everything to be had. So if you want something someone else has, you don't have to take his. All you need to do is work to get one of your own.

Della had that work ethic instilled in her by her parents, and, as an adult, she worked hard to provide her three daughters with all the things she'd lacked. She'd never had a prom dress or a birthday party or gifts at Christmas, and her sole focus in life was to give her girls everything. As she tearfully put it to me, "Those girls were the only reason I got up to go to work every day, to see to it they had everything they wanted." In fact, she was so single-minded in her devotion to her daughters that she'd lost two husbands because they resented the amount of attention she lavished on the children at their expense. Another

unforeseen result of Della's well-meaning but mis-
guided attempt to give her girls everything was that
they got to be so spoiled they simply assumed everything they had was theirs by right of birth.

Then, at the age of forty-two Della had a stroke. By
that time her daughters were grown and had families
of their own. Not one of them was willing to have
Della live with her, and the only person she had to depend on once her health failed was her cousin. The
girls' selfishness was heartbreaking to Della, who cried,
"What did I do wrong? I did all I could. I just don't
understand!"

I explained to Della that even though she'd given
them every material thing they could want or need,
the one thing she hadn't provided was the sense of responsibility her parents—despite everything they
couldn't give—had provided for her. She herself was
not a religious person because, she told me, the hard-
ships she'd endured as a child had taught her that she
had no one to depend on but herself. In counseling,
however, I was able to persuade her that even though
she'd abandoned God in her pursuit of worldly
goods—albeit it for her daughters rather than her-

self—He had not abandoned her. She may have been abandoned by her children, but as one of His children she would always be loved.

IS YOUR NEIGHBOR ENVIOUS OF YOU?

One of my pet philosophies—one that has made it much easier for me to avoid coveting what someone else has—is that, most of the time, when you want something another person has, you really think you want to be that person. When I spoke at career day at a local school a while back, I asked the students what they wanted to be when they grew up. In almost every instance, their answer involved being—or being "like"—someone else. "I want to sing like Beyoncé" or "I want to be a model like Tyra Banks" or "I want to live in a house like Kanye West's," or, plain and simple, "I want to be Oprah." I pointed out to them that it was great for them to take inspiration from these people, but that they also needed to think about being themselves—the best selves to which they could aspire.

If you think you want to be someone else, I would

ask you to consider this: Do you really know what was involved in that person's getting to be who he or she is? Do you know what struggles or sacrifices he made? Do you know what's really going on in his life?

If you did, you might not be so envious. And you also might want to consider whether the person of whom you are jealous mightn't also be jealous of you. Think about it. Have you ever said to someone, "Gee, I really envy you," only to have him reply, "You're kidding. I've always been jealous of you. You're so . . . (fill in the blank)."

I'll never forget Bea, who appeared to "have it all"—a beautiful home, a luxury car, fine jewelry, and a wardrobe filled with designer clothes. Everyone envied Bea, and family and friends often told her point blank, "Girl, I wish I had half of what you have." But behind her back people also remarked that she had a very high opinion of herself, and these remarks hurt Bea to the core. As she told me in counseling, "I'd give it all up gladly if I could have my old life back."

For twenty-three years Bea had been an average wife and mother who worked as a supervisor at a government agency. She and her family lived modestly, but they were comfortable and happy. Her husband was a good man and her two daughters were the joys of her life.

Then, one weekend, the family was planning to drive three hundred miles to visit her husband's mother and sister when, at the last minute, an emergency at work prevented Bea from making the trip. The rest of the family left on Friday afternoon and were planning to return on Sunday. Bea recalled the events of that Sunday eight years before as if they had happened yesterday. She was at home, awaiting their return, when the phone rang. The call was from a hospital informing her that there had been a serious accident involving a tractor-trailer and asking her to get to the hospital, which was less than an hour from her home, as quickly as possible. When she arrived, after a frantic drive, she was told that all three of them had been killed. She told me that she literally fainted from the shock and sobbed that "it still hurts."

People, she said, were kind and sympathetic. Afterward, there were so many details needing her attention that she took an extended leave of absence from her job. She sued the trucking company that owned the tractor-trailer whose driver had caused the accident, and after two years of legal wrangling, the case was settled for a large sum of money.

Bea said that since she had no one to leave it to, and because she now knew how uncertain life could be, she decided to spend it in whatever way she chose. Now, she told me, almost every conversation she had started with someone's saying, "If I had your money . . ." Some thoughtless individuals even remarked that "some people have all the luck." And many had the nerve to expect her to lend them money, clothing, or jewelry. On those few occasions when she went out socially with her friends, they expected her to pick up the tab.

"They want what I have?" Bea remarked bitterly. Do they also want the loneliness? Do they want to cry every night for eight years? Do they want to be haunted by images of their loved ones' mangled bodies?"

Bea couldn't understand why they would be envious of her, but God knew, from the very beginning, that envy and jealousy would stand between us and Him. He knew the danger of people's becoming so focused on the material world that they would lose sight of His divine guidance.

Bea, on the other hand, didn't realize that she too was covetous: She envied those who had husbands and children and grandchildren; she was jealous of other people's happiness. In counseling, I was able to help her see that there is always something to envy in others, and that she had no more reason to think that she knew any more about the inner lives of the people she envied than they did about hers. Only then was she able to understand the true meaning of the words in the Lord's Prayer that ask God to "forgive us our debts as we forgive our debtors," and to forgive not only her own envy but also those who envied her.

One of the problems with being obsessed by thoughts of what others have and we don't is that we fail to recognize or be grateful for what we do have. Take some time to stop and take stock of all your blessings and you may find that you have less reason to be envious.

JEALOUSY—THE GREEN-EYED MONSTER

Sometimes, it seems to me, people want things just so they can flaunt them. Do you remember the old Braniff airlines slogan, "If you've got it, flaunt it?" Do you also remember that Braniff went out of business? Acquiring something just so you can flaunt it means that the thing itself—whether it's a sable coat or a pair of sneakers—has no intrinsic value for you. What does this mean except the fact that you're piling up a lot of possessions whose only value lies in the eyes of others? The statement you're making is, "Look, see what I've got and you don't" and the implication is that, because you have it, you are somehow better than the person who doesn't.

And there's also a flip side to that coin. Sometimes people want something just because someone else has it. Maybe you've bought a new dress or a hat or a pair of shoes, and a few days later your friend turns up in the same item of clothing even though it might not suit him or her. Maybe you're flattered, but then again, you might wonder why this person made that purchase. Was it because he really thought you had such good taste or was it so that she could say, "See, I can have one, too"?

Envy has been called "the green-eyed monster," and one of the reasons given for the coining of that phrase is that green is a color associated with sickness. When you're sick, your skin often takes on a greenish pallor. What does that tell you? Envy is a sickness. It's a sickness of the mind and heart.

Maurice came to me for counseling because he knew that his envy was making him sick and bitter. He was a hard worker with a good job as a mechanic working on luxury automobiles. When he shared his life story with me, I learned that his father had abandoned the family when Maurice was eleven years old and left his mother to raise him and his two sisters. They were always struggling to make ends meet and Maurice worked after school to contribute to the family income. He recalled bitterly that he hadn't been able to play on his high school basketball team because his job interfered with practices and he hadn't gone to his prom because his mother said there wasn't any money to waste on such frivolities.

After graduating from high school, he'd begun, as he put it, to "mess around" with cars and had gone to trade school to earn his mechanic's certification. His one fantasy in life was to own a car like the ones he now worked on, and he envied those who drove them to the point of hatred. "What did they do to deserve living high on the hog?" he demanded. He realized that his envy was becoming obsessive and that it was crazy to hate people he didn't even know, but he simply couldn't help himself. These negative feelings were making his life miserable and he was having trouble dealing with his emotions. It wasn't only their cars that he envied; he also coveted their attractive wives and their beautiful homes. He envied them their jobs and was angry that he didn't have a job where he could wear a suit and tie to work.

Of course, I shared with him the destructive power of jealousy and reminded him that he didn't really know what it had taken for the people he envied to get what they had. For all he knew they had worked and sacrificed to buy what they owned and had missed out on other pleasures along the way. In fact, I told him, I knew a young man who had the car Maurice dreamed of owning. He'd bought it with the insurance money he received after his parents had died in a house fire and he would have gladly returned the car if that would bring his parents back.

Maurice laughed when I suggested that people might be envious of his skill as a mechanic or the booming tenor voice that had earned him a place in his church choir, and I suggested that he begin to express more gratitude for what he did have.

When I asked him to focus on the one thing he wanted more than any other, he immediately responded that it was the car. I recalled the old saying, "Where there's a will, there's a way," and suggested that he begin seeking a way to get what his heart desired. He didn't think prayer was going to help because he'd been praying for a decent car for years, but I told him that it was a mistake to pray for a particular thing rather than for the guidance and opportunity to achieve it.

He admitted that his way hadn't worked so far, so I suggested that it was time to try something new. I told him to read the Bible and look for stories of people who had overcome adversity to achieve success. He canceled his next two sessions, but when he finally reappeared he was grinning from ear to ear. He directed me to "look out the window," and there at the curb was parked a beautiful luxury car.

Maurice told me that he'd done what I recommended and, in a conversation with one of his customers, had learned that there were auctions where cars were sold far below market price. The customer volunteered to take Maurice to the next auction he attended, and that's where he'd bid on and bought his new car. Although it was preowned, Maurice knew that it was in great condition and he intended to keep it that way. He also intended to go to more auctions, buy more cars, and resell them at a profit. Now he had a plan, not just a daydream, and for the first time in his life he actually felt good about himself.

If you follow God's commandment, you won't have to make yourself sick with envy. Enjoy what you have in a spirit of gratitude. And if you trust in God as He wants you to, you will know that by obeying Him, you will prosper.

NOT EVERYTHING WE COVET IS
MATERIAL IN NATURE

Throughout the ages, there are those who have coveted power and prestige, status and influence. In fact, one of the reasons people covet wealth is that, in their eyes, money means power. In fact, they often get pleasure from the fact that those who have less or whom they consider inferior, hate them. In their own sick minds, these people love being hated! Instead of using money for the good, too many of us use it only to bend others to our will or to flaunt our "buying power." These days we hear a lot about people "buying loyalty" or "buying" another person's silence. We're all familiar with the words of Paul's First Epistle in Timothy 6:10, "The love of money is the root of all evil," and it's certainly true that those who put money before the Lord are likely to have "pierced themselves through with many sorrows." But it is equally against the will of God to misuse what money we have.

Money, however, isn't the only way to gain power and prestige, and sometimes it's simply the status we covet, regardless of monetary gain. Glenda, a professional acquaintance of mine, was one who coveted titles and the prestige they bestowed. She would go to any lengths to thwart anyone whom she perceived as a rival or a threat to the fulfillment of her ambitions. At one time she and another applicant, who was also a friend, were being considered for the same position. Glenda knew the other applicant was more qualified, but, as Glenda put it, she wanted the job so badly she could taste it. What she really wanted, however, was not the responsibility that went with the position; rather, she wanted the title, the corporate car, being able to fly first class to meetings, and the staff that would be under her supervision. And she wanted to flaunt all these perks in the faces of those who had passed her over for promotion in the past.

To get what she wanted, Glenda broke another of God's commandments: She bore false witness against her rival by starting a rumor about her that was, in fact, a vicious lie. Her scheme, unfortunately, worked, and Glenda got the job. But her lack of qualifications soon became evident and she was let go just four months later.

Shortly after her termination, Glenda was diagnosed with ovarian cancer and, as the illness progressed, was confined to a nursing home where her "friend" and erstwhile rival sat by her side day after day. Finally Glenda confessed what she had done, told the other woman how sorry she was, and asked for her forgiveness.

As it turned out, her friend said that she had known all along, but she had been blessed with an even better position and was extremely content. As a result, she bore Glenda no ill will.

"I was blessed," Glenda said, "but did not appreciate what I had or who I was." However, she believed that she had been forgiven by God as well as her friend, both of whom were with her until the end.

ASK AND IT SHALL BE GIVEN YOU

When Christ came to earth he gave man the formula for success: "Ask and it shall be given you; seek and ye shall find; knock, and it shall be opened unto you: For every one that asketh receiveth; and he that seeketh findeth; and to him that knocketh it shall be opened" (Matthew 7:7–8).

The problem is that most people "ask" as a form of wishful thinking and in fleeting moments of prayer. But it doesn't work that way. We must ask while having faith that God will hear us. "Seek ye first the kingdom of God, and his righteousness; and all these things shall be added unto you" (Matthew 6:33). What this means is that we must put God first, and if we do that, He will provide the "add ons."

I have many friends who pass along e-mail containing pithy sayings and powerful truths. This is one of my favorites:

To get something you never had, you have to do something you never did.

When God takes something from your grasp, He's not punishing you, but merely opening your hand to receive something better.

The will of God will never take you where the grace of God will not protect you.

COMMANDING THOUGHTS

• Is there someone of whom you are jealous or envious? If so, why?

- What satisfaction do you get from harboring these feelings?

- Do you have a lustful nature?

- Have you thought about how these negative thoughts might be hindering your success?

- Are you grateful for who you are and what you have?

- Why not let go and let God's will be done in your life.

CHAPTER ELEVEN

CLEAN UP THE MESS AND GET RID OF THE STRESS

"The devil can cite Scripture for his purpose."

—WILLIAM SHAKESPEARE, *The Merchant of Venice*

Not too long ago, I decided to look up the word *mess* in my dictionary. The first definition was "an unappetizing, disagreeable concoction," followed by "a state of disorder," "trouble," and "embarrassment," "a confused mass of things," "jumble," and "hodgepodge." Thinking about those definitions, I decided that they were all relevant to the times we live in. Messy, disagreeable, disordered scenarios are playing out daily in this country and all over the world. But the messy state of the world does not justify the personal messes we make of our lives.

For some people life is, indeed, an unappetizing,

disagreeable concoction; others live in an ongoing state of disorder and trouble. The reason, I believe, for the messes we are experiencing as individuals and society as a whole, is that things are out of divine order and mankind has rebelled against the commandments of God. When God made man, He had a plan—a plan that would bless His creation, not create the mess we see today.

STOP THE SPREAD OF THE MESS

A mess may begin like a tiny pulled thread in the fabric of our life, and then, before we know it, that tiny flaw unravels more and more until the whole thing is coming to pieces. And, like any other initially indiscernible but critical flaw, the bigger it gets the harder it becomes to mend. So, if you find your life unraveling because of some mess of your own creation, I would suggest that it's a good idea to start making amends right now.

The more the messes in our lives escalate, the more stressed and powerless we become. It is time to start looking for more stability and order in our lives. God didn't create His laws to restrict us; rather they were designed to empower and liberate us from our own human fallibility. God knew we were fallible, and so He gave us His guidelines to prevent us from having to stress about every decision and make unnecessary mistakes.

THINK STRAIGHT TO WALK
A STRAIGHT LINE

You can't think crooked and walk straight, but if your mind is properly focused, the rest of you will follow. Many of the messes in our lives result from the individual choices we make, so changing the way we think will change the way we behave.

The Bible tells us that, "as he [or she] thinketh in his [her] heart, so *is* he [she]" (Proverbs 23:7). If our thoughts are focused on following a moral, Godly path, that's the path we'll walk; but if we're not focused on following His lead, we are very likely to be led astray.

Sadly, in many families today, low expectations have proven to be detrimental to advancement and spiritual growth. It makes one shudder to hear the limited verbal skills of many people of our time. But for some strange reason, they can curse and take God's name in vain fluently. I remember well when being "bad" brought shame and dishonor to one's family and the family name. But today, being called "bad" is almost a badge of honor. Young people are known to say, "I got my bad on" or, "Hey! you bad."

When dealing with a group of inner city youth, I found it difficult and challenging to communicate with them out of the bounds of their coded vocabulary. So, I encouraged them to be "B.A.A.D." I redefined BAAD as,

B—begin

A—again

A—and

D—determined

I also encouraged them to try being BAAD in a positive way. For youths and adults alike, God extends to all the opportunity to begin again. If you have not tried to live by or pattern your life after God's law, now is a good time to try it and to inspire others to do likewise.

A prime example of someone who couldn't walk straight because she didn't know which way to turn was my client Tammy. Tammy was a certified public accountant in her midthirties working for a major corporation. When she arrived for her first appointment—a half hour late—she was impeccably made up and dressed to the nines but I could tell immediately that she was physically and mentally drained and exhausted. Her first words to me were, "I am just stressed out. I don't even know if I'm coming or going." And she then informed me that she'd been enrolled in courses dealing with money management, anger management, and time management. She confessed that even though her job involved managing money for other people, her own finances were a mess. She was temperamental and, in her own words, tended to "fly off the handle" when aggravated. She'd been reprimanded more than once for being late in delivering her reports.

Tammy's lament was that there simply weren't enough hours in the day for her to complete all her professional responsibilities and she had absolutely no time to look after herself or do things she enjoyed. During our first couple of sessions she was text-messaging during our conversations, checking messages on her BlackBerry, and excusing herself to make cell phone calls. I informed her that this was unacceptable and that if she was serious about dealing with her problems she'd have to give our sessions her undivided attention.

Although her medical history indicated that she was in good health, she was hyperventilating, talking too fast, and had difficulties remaining focused. Her friends, she said, had suggested that she try Yoga, an exercise regime, or even a modern dance class to help relieve her stress, but Tammy complained that adding another obligation to her already overflowing plate just made her even more stressed. Whenever I meet someone like Tammy I'm reminded of the words, "Be still, and know that I *am* God" (Psalms 46:10). I suggested that she try taking deep breaths, a strategy that has been shown to relieve tension and ward off panic attacks.

My first assignment for Tammy was to list all the things she had to do, the things she chose to do, and those she could eliminate from her daily life. I told her to bring the list with her the next time she came so that we could analyze it together. When Tammy arrived the following week I was amused to see that she seemed embarrassed to show me her list. She'd scribbled over, crossed-out, rearranged, and switched priorities from one list to another. She seemed to be clear on what she had to do, but she was vague on what she wanted to do and couldn't really decide what she'd be able to eliminate.

After reviewing the list, I said, "Tammy, you've left God out completely, and it's Him you need most to relieve your stress." In addition to excluding God, Tammy had neglected to mention reading, meditating, worship, or doing anything for others.

People like Tammy often neglect to apply God's law to their lives. The Bible instructs us to "In all thy ways acknowledge him, and he shall direct thy paths." (Proverbs 3:6). And further, we are reminded in Corinthians that, "your body is the temple of the Holy Ghost *which is* in you, which ye have of God. . . . therefore glorify God in your body, and in your spirit, which are God's" (1 Corinthians 6:19–20). Tammy was not only putting everything in her life before God, she was also dishonoring Him by neglecting her health.

At one point she admitted that she slept about only five hours a night. Like so many of us, she went to bed tired and woke up tired, and because she was always playing catch-up in her life, she neglected to honor His commandment to observe the Sabbath.

With time, she did make changes. She learned to turn off her cell phone and BlackBerry in the evening and on weekends. She cut back on the time she spent selecting a wardrobe and applying her makeup each morning. And she joined a group therapy session made up of others like her who were trying to reduce their levels of stress. After a couple of months she shared with me that, although it had been difficult for her to make the changes, she was feeling a lot less stressed.

IF YOU OPEN THE DOOR
THE DEVIL WILL ENTER

When we're stressed and overwhelmed it's easy to open a door in our heart for the devil to enter. The late comedian Flip Wilson got a lot of laughs with his patented excuse, "The devil made me do it." And back in the 1950s and '60s many African American churches featured a play in which the devil tempted people to do wrong and then pitched them into hell. The play was amusing but its message was also thought-provoking.

We may depict the devil as a cartoonlike character dressed in red with pointy ears and a pitchfork in hand, but he is, in fact, a force that would like nothing more than to replace God in our heart. His main weapon is temptation and the main thrust of his agenda is to get us to disobey just one of God's commandments because, as a fallen angel, he knows that once we begin to slide there's no stopping our descent into disobedience.

He even had the audacity to tempt Jesus himself. As is recounted in Matthew 4:5–10, "Then the devil taketh him up into the holy city, and setteth him on a pinnacle of the temple, And saith unto him, If thou be the Son of God, cast thyself down: for it is written, He shall give his angels charge concerning thee; and in *their* hands they shall bear thee up, lest at any time thou dash thy foot against a stone. Jesus said unto him, It is written again, Thou shalt not tempt the Lord thy God. Again, the devil taketh him up into an exceeding high mountain, and sheweth him all the kingdoms of the world, and the glory of them; And saith unto him, All these things will I give thee, if thou wilt fall down and worship me. Then saith Jesus unto him, Get thee hence, Satan: for it is written, Thou shalt worship the Lord thy God, and him only shalt thou serve."

He's a clever devil, cunning and deceitful, and he knows our fleshly desires, so we must be careful not to make room for him in our heart. If our heart is filled with love for God the devil cannot enter, for he is incapable of love. But if we allow him, he will weasel and connive to win us over, and then he will destroy us. Satan is evil, and we are all capable of evil. But we are also empowered by God to resist temptation. So as long as we walk with Him in our heart we need fear no evil. "Submit yourselves therefore to God. Resist the devil, and he will flee from you" (James 4:7).

IN WEAKNESS THERE IS STRENGTH

There are too many among us who think that they "know it all" and consider themselves experts on the facts of life. They believe they are strong enough to walk without God as a guide. But, as we learn in Matthew 23:12, "Whosoever shall exalt himself shall be abased; and he that shall humble himself shall be exalted." And, in Proverbs 1:7, "The fear of the Lord *is* the beginning of knowledge: *but* fools despise wisdom and instruction."

It always amuses me when people equate fearing God with being afraid of what He might do to punish them. To fear God in the true spiritual sense is to revere Him, respect Him, and love Him with all your heart. He is a loving God who gave us the Ten Commandments as a blueprint for success. But in the Parable of the Unfaithful Servant, who "knew his lord's will, and prepared not *himself*, neither did according to his will," we learn that "unto whomsoever much is given, of him shall be much required" (Luke 12:47, 48). We are the Lord's servants, and He expects much of us. If we choose not to honor the gifts He has given us by showing our love and respect for His blueprint, we are, in fact, choosing to build a life that is headed for destruction.

If, on the other hand, we put ourselves in His hands and admit our weakness, He will give us strength. In times past, our fore-parents seemed to handle stress better than we do today. Despite the burdens they carried, they had a blessed assurance that whatever their needs, God would provide. They truly believed, as we are told in Psalms 27:1, that, "The Lord *is* the strength of my life; of whom shall I be afraid?"

Traditionally, in the African American culture God's warriors delighted in reminiscing about how "Joshua fought the battle of Jericho and the walls came tumbling down." They raised their voices in praise, singing "I'm a Soldier in the Army of the Lord." Nowadays, however, spiritual weakness is reflected in a lack of mental and physical resilience. People are so overwhelmed by stress that they wind up crying out, "I can't take it anymore." What these people need to understand is that God did not intend us to stand on our own. As He told Saint Paul, "My grace is sufficient for thee: for my strength is made perfect in weakness"

(2 Corinthians 12:9), causing Paul to respond, "Most gladly therefore will I rather glory in my infirmities, that the power of Christ may rest upon me. Therefore I take pleasure in infirmities, in reproaches, in necessities, in persecutions, in distresses for Christ's sake: for when I am weak, then am I strong" (2 Corinthians 12:9–10). God fortifies us with both physical and spiritual strength.

FOR GOD NOTHING IS IMPOSSIBLE

When Mary, still a virgin, was told by the angel that she would become pregnant with the Son of God, and also that her cousin Elizabeth, who had been considered barren, was expecting a child, Mary wondered how these things could be and was told by the angel, "with God nothing shall be impossible" (Luke 1:37).

It has been said that God makes impossibilities possible, but, sadly, there are those who do not give God a chance to show them what is possible. When we choose not to allow Him to direct our lives, we are depriving ourselves of His power to accelerate our success.

COMMANDING THOUGHTS

- Is your mind cluttered with negativity?

- Begin a mental and spiritual purging process.

- Are you prepared for a faith-focused future?

- Avoid messy situations.

- Have you dismissed from your life people who are constantly involving you in their mess?

- Remember: mess won't be blessed.

CHAPTER TWELVE

USE THE POWER OF THE 10 TO ACHIEVE SUCCESS

"Everybody finds out sooner or later that all success worth having is founded on Christian rules of conduct."

—HENRY MARTYN FIELD, author and clergyman

How do you define success? The dictionary offers several choices, among them "the attainment of wealth, position, honors, or the like." Certainly there are many among us who would define success in these terms. Others talk about having a successful marriage or having undergone a successful medical procedure. People refer to a party or a special event as having been an overwhelming success. But these are all secondary manifestations of what is, in fact, the first dictionary definition: "The favorable or prosperous termination of attempts or endeavors." I would, therefore, propose that the true road to success is to live a life according to the laws of the Lord, which will surely lead us to the favorable outcomes of all our endeavors.

God gave us the gifts that are the keys to true success. As it says in 2 Timothy 1:6–7: "Wherefore I put thee in remembrance, that thou stir up the gift of God, which is in thee by the putting on of my hands. For God hath not given us the spirit of fear; but of power, and of love, and of a sound mind." To achieve success we must lay aside fear of failure and keep the power of God's love in our mind at all times.

Sometimes people who consider themselves successful chalk it up to luck. We've all heard people claim that they're "lucky in love," or, when we ask them to what they attribute their success, that they're "just lucky, I guess." True success, however, requires much more than luck. It requires having a vision of what God wants of and for us. "Where *there is* no vision, the people perish: but he that keepeth the law, happy *is* he" (Proverbs 29:18). With that vision firmly embedded in our heart, we have access to His power.

THE ONLY TRUE POWER
BELONGS TO GOD

We live in an age where everything runs on power; if there's a power failure, our lives virtually come to a halt. When your cell phone battery runs out of power it's like losing a lifeline. The United States boasts of its military power, but as more and more lives are lost, that power is diminished. People run for political office to achieve power, but when they're defeated in the next election, they're out of power. Many people believe that money is power, but money that is made can also be lost.

I have known many people who schemed—and often scammed—their entire life to achieve wealth and power. One of those was a memorable character appropriately named Wynn (or, at least, that's what I'm going to call him). From an early age, Wynn was determined to become a millionaire and a power broker. He made it his business to meet and mingle with the rich and powerful and to emulate their style. He was a savvy guy and a true wheeler-dealer, and by the time he was in his midthirties he had made his millions in real estate development and what looked like smart investments.

Wynn enjoyed his wealth, buying himself a big fancy house, a yacht, and membership in an exclusive country club. He also married a lovely young socialite befitting his social status. He was featured in many articles about successful African Americans and was even invited to the White House. Politicians sought his endorsement and, of course, his generous campaign contributions.

Wynn thought his luxurious life would last forever, but after a good nine-year run living high off the hog, his financial empire began to crumble. It turned out that he owed hundreds of thousands of dollars in back taxes, and he didn't have the money to pay off his debt. He was overextended and creditors were reluctant to throw good money after bad. And he also discovered that many of the items for which he'd spent top dollar were worth a lot less than he'd paid. He hired a high-priced legal team that further drained his resources and still he lost his case. The IRS immediately put a lien on his properties and confiscated all his remaining assets.

Wynn's wife, who was a strong woman, believed that her husband was contemplating suicide and brought him to me for counseling. "I had it all, and now it's gone," he cried, weeping unashamedly. "I just can't go on. I can't start over. What do I have to live for?" This was clearly a broken man, who also bemoaned the fact that many of those he had helped in the past now avoided his phone calls and he was no longer invited to the parties he had previously sponsored.

He and his wife had moved from their McMansion to a modest two-bedroom apartment, which, for Wynn, felt like living in the slums. He no longer believed in God and told me that praying and attending church were both out of the question. Knowing that I was a Christian counselor, he sarcastically suggested that if I could "get a prayer through," maybe I could pray for him. Of course, I told Wynn that prayers weren't magic and, moreover, that they weren't meant to ask for material things. I suggested that he pray for the strength and power to see him through hard times, but Wynn's response to that was, "I don't want the strength to live as a failure. I want to be rich and successful again."

Just reviewing his life with me was extremely painful. Wynn had defined himself entirely by what he had rather than who he was, and he'd never imagined that anything in his life could change. It took me several sessions to get through to him, but I gradually got him to admit that he'd been irresponsible in the way he'd handled his finances, and that was devastating to him.

When I asked him to tell me who he really was without the success and power he'd once wielded, he told me that he thought he was worthless. I recited a few affirmations, which he consented to repeat half-heartedly: "I need God in my life. God is the God of second chances. I am grateful for having experienced success, wealth, and power. I will ask the Lord for forgiveness and I will forgive myself."

I firmly believe that we can always begin again, but a new beginning should not be the attempt to repeat or retrieve what was lost. Rather it should be looked at as an opportunity to explore new avenues.

I reminded him of the verse in the twenty-third Psalm that says, "He restoreth my soul," and Wynn ruefully told me that he knew the psalm very well. I then suggested that we move on to restoring his lost faith in both God and himself and assured him once again that God truly wanted us to succeed but that there was more to success than the accumulation of wealth and power.

His homework assignment was to reread the Ten Commandments and think about what place they had in his life. When he came to our next session, Wynn told me that he knew he'd placed everything else in his life before God and that the things he had loved were not capable of returning his love. He also realized that during his years of success he hadn't really established any meaningful friendships. All those he had deemed his friends were really business associates and acquaintances who had used him—as he had used them—to further their agendas.

The one shining star in Wynn's life was his wife. When her mother died and left her a small inheritance, she used the money to help Wynn open a small business advising entrepreneurs on how to obtain funding. The business grew by word of mouth and gradually Wynn regained some financial stability. He's proud of the fact that he's been much more successful advising others than he'd been with his own fortune, and he's no longer driven to regain his reputation as the poster boy for African American success.

There's only one kind of power that is never lost and never runs out, and that is the power of the Lord, which He, out of love, shares with His children, asking only that we obey His laws.

REMEMBER TO PUT GOD'S LAWS FIRST

The Ten Commandments are not God's suggestions or recommendations: They are His laws. And yet there are many among us who claim to love God but question or even ignore His laws. This is nothing new; it's been going on since biblical times. As Jesus told the Pharisees in Mark 7:6–8, recalling the prophesy of Isaiah, "This people honoreth me with *their* lips, but their heart is far from me. Howbeit in vain do they worship me, teaching *for* doctrines the commandments of men.

For laying aside the commandment of God, ye hold the tradition of men."

Today we put the traditions of men above the laws of God by turning holy days into holidays. We celebrate the birth of Christ with Santa Claus, reindeer, greeting cards, and parties. We remember his resurrection with Easter egg hunts, gift baskets, and fancy new hats. And we observe the Sabbath by sleeping late, shopping, and watching sports on television instead of going to church.

By ignoring His laws we forfeit His power to help us. We listen to the fallible opinions of our fellow men instead of the infallible wisdom of God. We boast of being self-made men (and women), but what have we made of ourselves but sinners in the eyes of the Lord? Kind David, who was by any standard one of the most successful people of his time, was guilty of sin and could not enjoy his worldly achievements knowing that he had failed God. In Psalm 51:12 he pleads with God to "restore unto me the joy of thy salvation; and uphold me *with thy* free spirit."

LET YOUR GOAL BE SPIRITUAL SUCCESS

If you make spiritual success the destination of your life's journey you may encounter detours and delays, but if you keep your eye on the end of the road, God will be there to guide you. Keep telling yourself, "I can do all things through Christ which strengtheneth me" (Philippians 4:13). And covenant with the Creator that as you are blessed, so will you bless others.

There may be times when others try to force you off your chosen path, and when that happens you need to hold it close to your heart. Do things decently and, as Spike Lee put it, "Do the right thing."

I remember an occasion many years ago when I was applying for a particular position. I'd sent out a number of résumés and had several interviews without result. I knew I was capable and qualified, but for some reason I was facing one rejection after another.

I just kept repeating to myself, "What I am looking for is looking for me." Knowing that faith sometimes requires patience and perseverance, I never gave up. Then one day I was on a plane returning home from a conference in Seattle, Washington, when the gentleman in the seat next to me struck up a conversation and asked me about my profession. I explained what I did, and he immediately exclaimed, "What a coincidence. I'm looking for someone with exactly your qualifications." It turned out that he was the CEO of a major corporation with whom I would never have gotten an interview if I'd gone through traditional channels. He gave me his card and when I got home I made an appointment to see him. He hired me and I enjoyed representing his company throughout the United States and in several foreign countries for the next five years.

Be calm and courageous. Listen to that small voice within and take risks when they are necessary. Keep affirming to yourself, "I will be successful in all my undertakings," and do not confuse success with money and power. Remember that success is the favorable outcome of all your endeavors.

COMMANDING THOUGHTS

• Do you have a plan for success?

• What is the source of your power to achieve?

- Do you believe in yourself?

- Are your goals realistic?

- Are you prepared to fail before you succeed?

- How will your success benefit others?

- Don't forget to pray before pursuing your goal.

- Keep faith and keep victory in view.

IN CLOSING

I've written this book in the hope that it will help you to reflect on your life and your relationship with your Creator, the Almighty God.

All that is required for you to establish, renew, or revise that relationship is for you to take the leap of faith and know that by living in obedience to His commandments you will be harnessing the power they hold.

If you find that your life is full of drama and discontent, why not try something old instead of something new. God's instructions for living have stood the test of time, and they have never been known to fail. You abide by thousands of laws governing everything that you do every day, so why not include the original ten?

The Ten Commandments were designed not to bind you but to set you free from the bonds and consequences you bring on yourself through disobedience.

They continue to prevail because they have eternal power:

The power of truth

The power of love

The power of divine direction

The power of faith

The power of joy

The power of peace

The power of relationship with God

The power of prayer

The power of forgiveness

The power of God's power

ACKNOWLEDGMENTS

The writing of this book occurred during the most challenging period of my life. I was diagnosed with severe glaucoma that impacted and reduced my vision, and faced the possibility of becoming totally blind. Faith became my main source of strength, and I refused to accept that possibility. I never experienced depression or fear, but my patience was tested beyond measure. I found strength in knowing that "They that wait upon the Lord shall renew *their* strength" (Isaiah 40:31).

I was blessed with a circle of encouragers, people who prayed for me and who dared me to give up or accept defeat by not completing this project. I recalled a line in a hymn that says "Lord, haste the day when my faith shall be sight," and that day finally arrived!

I acknowledge with overwhelming gratitude the support and encouragement of Janet Hill-Talbert, formerly of Doubleday, and her husband, Aaron; Barbara Lowenstein and Madeleine Morel, my agents and beloved Jewish sisters; Judy Kern, my editor, who is without doubt the best in the business, and her canine baby girl, Katie. I would also like to thank Christian Nwachukwu, Jr., of Doubleday for his faith in me; Elizabeth and William Stewart, my friends for life; my godsons, Reverend Joseph Jackson, Jr., and Reverend Kenneth D. Clayton; Professor Caffie Risher, my daughter in Ministry; and Linda Graves, for those late-night phone calls of encouragement. I am grateful to Dr. Betty Martin-Blount for her friendship and research; Chenise Lytrelle Williams, my goddaughter and personal poet; Reverend Britt Starghill and Bishop André Jackson; Willida Harris Luff, my sister; and my son, Lenord Arlen Churn.

Many thanks also to my clients whose stories I share with those who read this book. I have gone to great lengths to protect their identities while telling their stories to benefit others.

Lastly, my deepest appreciation is extended to Delores A. Rush, my administrator, who has been by my side daily. She was my eyes when I could not see and has been there for me and with me every step of the way. Her friendship is my daily blessing from God.

ABOUT THE AUTHOR

An ordained Baptist minister and certified Grief Counsel Specialist, the Rev. Arlene Churn, Ph.D., served as Plenary Chair of the White House Conference on Children and as coordinator of the 3.5 million female members of the National Baptist Convention, USA, Inc. Currently president of Unlimited Horizons, a consulting firm, she travels around the globe as an acclaimed motivational speaker. She lives in Philadelphia, Pennsylvania.